Slacklands 2

Slacklands 2

Corinna Dean

A guide to Rural Contemporary Architecture
of the Twentieth Century

Slacklands is a guide to Rural Contemporary Architecture
of the Twentieth Century. The guidebook provides a tour of rural
structures and their surrounding territories navigating through
Cold War relics and functional buildings. Slacklands provides
a portal on the poetic and aesthetically daring structures that
have left indelible marks on the global landscape.

Contents

Foreword   7
Charles Holland

Introduction   16
Corinna Dean

Cold War and Military Sites

Satcom II Satellite Ground Listening Station	38
Maritime Museum	42
Cold War Military Camp	44
Former Radar Station and Missile Base	52
Roadblock	54
Pillbox in Former Monastic Building	56
Gun Battery	60
Atlantic Wall	62
Langham Dome	64
Manston Airfield	68
Bombing Decoy	74
Casabianca Battery	76
Favignana Bunker	80

Modern Follies and Religious Buildings

La Stella	98
Spanish Chapel	102
Crystal Palace Concert Pavilion	106
St Paul's Church	110

Functional Buildings

Headframe of the Sainte Marie Coalmine	126
Curtis's & Harvey Ltd Explosives Factory	128
Dingleton Boiler	134
Backwater Reservoir	136
Water Tower	140
Stewartby Brickworks	142
Caminito del Rey	148
Iznájar Dam	150
Bernat Klein Studio	154

Architecture of Leisure

Bentota Beach Hotel	170
Gala Fairydean Stadium	176
Las Cabañas	178
Olau Passenger Ferry	182
Cliftonville Lido	186
The Colonia Principi di Piemonte	188

Foreword

Charles Holland

The cult of the ruin is a peculiarly British obsession, one that can be traced back at least as far as the picturesque tradition of building follies, grottoes and ruins in the gardens of country houses. This was in turn influenced by the Grand Tour and an aristocratic experience of the ruins of Greek and Roman culture. Imported back to England, these romantic ruins were underpinned by the spoils of a new, mercantile empire.

Corinna Dean's first *Slacklands* book updated this tradition but with very different protagonists: military, industrial and municipal buildings from the twentieth century. Power Stations, factories, jetties and pill boxes offer a kind of contemporary Grand Tour, one where obsolescence results from changing technologies, shifts in government policy and the cross-currents of geo-politics. Despite its obsession with the (recent) past, *Slacklands* tapped into a very current feeling for the history of ordinary spaces and an interest in the previously overlooked corners of our world.

I recently visited Dungeness in Kent on a sunny spring weekend. On the face of it, Dungeness is a very *Slacklands* kind of place: bleak, isolated and loomed over by a vast nuclear power station. It is as far from a traditional beauty spot as one could imagine. And yet on this May afternoon it was busy, cars parked nose to tail by the side of the road and the pub and sea food shop both doing brisk business. This is a new form of tourism, one informed by landscape writing, contemporary art and psychogeography and drawn to marginal places and the sidenotes of traditional history.

There is a danger then that the off-piste exploration becomes the well-trodden path. Or that we end up engaging in a twenty-first century version of Victorian sentimentalism, dishevelled farm cottages replaced by the ruins of social democracy. But *Slacklands* is admirably unsentimental and matter-of-fact in tone. It has a depth of interest in these marginal spaces that makes the book closer to a taxonomy of redundancy than a guidebook for the ruin-porn enthusiast. It is an inventory that keeps growing too, expanding its remit to include – in this second book – Geoffrey Bawa's hotel in Sri Lanka, an abandoned mineshaft (is there any other kind?) in France and a former military camp in Albania.

Slacklands is part of a wider project. It is one that challenges traditional notions of beauty and value, a non-aggrandising form of history that is interested in failure, obsolescence and even ugliness. It also acknowledges an important truth about the countryside, which, far from being an unspoilt rural arcadia, is in fact riddled with the detritus of nineteenth and twentieth century technology. Binary oppositions between the urban and the rural often fail to acknowledge the presence of each in the other. It is good to see the ambiguous spaces and places in between celebrated.

Slacklands may be grounded in an objective desire to reveal places as they really are, but it leaves plenty of room for poetry. The buildings it records are sufficiently obscure to allow personal interpretation and a sense of discovery. It will show you things you didn't know and take you places you haven't been. Enjoy the journey.

Introduction

Corinna Dean

Slacklands 2 expands on the first collection of buildings in the first edition published in 2014, categorised under four typologies – Military Sites, Modern Follies and Religious Buildings, Functional Buildings and Leisure, as well as broadening the reach of sites. My interest in rural structures and their surrounding landscapes was sparked by journeys as a child out of Edinburgh along the A1 east coast route. Speeding past Torness Power station the façade of the reactor hall shimmered and radiated like a bar of gold, hit by the setting sun, smack into the west facing façade. My mother would highlight this odd choice of building teasingly pointing out 'there's Corinna's favourite building'.

The combination of the sun's radiation to augment the building's façade and the knowledge later of how nuclear fusion worked, as well as a visit to its interior before visitors were banned post 9/11, made the building appear even more intriguing. Here was one of the most potentially deadly processes sitting upon a unique and remodeled landscape, not far from the majestic Bass Rock, a volcanic plug; processes, deep and potentially deadly were behind what was essentially a piece of technology housed in a shed.

It is nearly 50 years since the cultural theorist, Paul Virilio set out on the Atlantic Coast, on a journey of curiosity equipped only with his camera to visit the World War Two coastal defence structures. Fifty years on, these bunkers are weathered, their contours engrained by the prevailing winds. More importantly

↗
The Water Tower sits 40 km
south of Cochin, Kerala.

↘
The bunker is one of thousands that still pepper both urban and rural areas of Albania. It is reputed that for every square kilometre there are 5.7 bunkers.

← The weathered bunker sits on the Aeolian island, Favignana just off the Sicilian coast.

their concrete structures are being broken down, mixed with sand particles, shedding layers slowly but significantly. Eventually the fine aggregate of sand, cement and ballast will begin to compact with natural sedimentation and make up a new layer of geographical strata, one which will contribute to the earth's layers more than natural elements. Concrete can make the dubious claim to be the most representative material of the Anthropocene and with this perhaps darker veil, I chose to frame the sites – one which situates the buildings and their context in what has been labelled 'deep time'.

It was between the years 1958–1965 when Virilio took the images of the bunkers along the littoral coast, presented at an exhibition at the *Museum of Decorative Arts*, Paris, 1975. The catalogue accompanying the show, titled *Bunker Archeology* described, his objective as 'solely archaeological'. Describing what first drew his attention to these structures, Virilio muses that it was a combination of 'a case of intuition' and also as a convergence between the reality of the structure and the fact of its implementation alongside the coast, creating an awareness of spatial phenomena, 'They provoked cultural memories prompting thoughts of Egyptian mastabas, Etruscan tombs, Aztec structures almost funeral type ceremony'.

The past decade or so has seen a revisiting of these structures and similar clones along the UK coast line culminating in a contemporary obsession with ruins borne out in the

→
The modest building with its bricked up windows sits on the former dynamite factory site on the Hoo Peninsula, Medway.

exhibition titled *Ruin Lust* (2014), at London's *Tate Britain* gallery. This fascination is very different from the architect Joseph Gandy's painting of a fantasy ruin of John Soane's 'Bank of England' with the City of London imagined as a swampy wilderness, an early pre-emption of the artist Robert Smithson's reading of time as ruins in reverse. Smithson viewed twentieth century infrastructure and the environment as relics that 'don't fall into ruin after they are built but rather rise into ruin before they are built', disrupting our sense of time and our reading of time as a romantic notion.

Slacklands 2 expands beyond buildings of a military nature to include a French mine shaft which sits in the shadow of Le Corbusier's Ronchamp Chapel, to a former brickworks and a derelict Geoffrey Bawa hotel in Sri Lanka. Many of the structures have been reclaimed by the elements. Bunkers have been allowed to slip unceremoniously off cliffs or sandbanks. The weather is visibly tattooed onto their surface. In the case of the military sites, it is not just their readings as brutalist relics of war that are celebrated but also a focus upon the vitality of the buildings' material and their hosting of sub species, such as algae, lichen and the ecological shifts in landscapes in which they stand.

↗
The welcoming gateway monument stands at the entrance to Gibellina Nuova, one of many bold public art commissions in the new town in Sicily.

Cold War and Military Sites

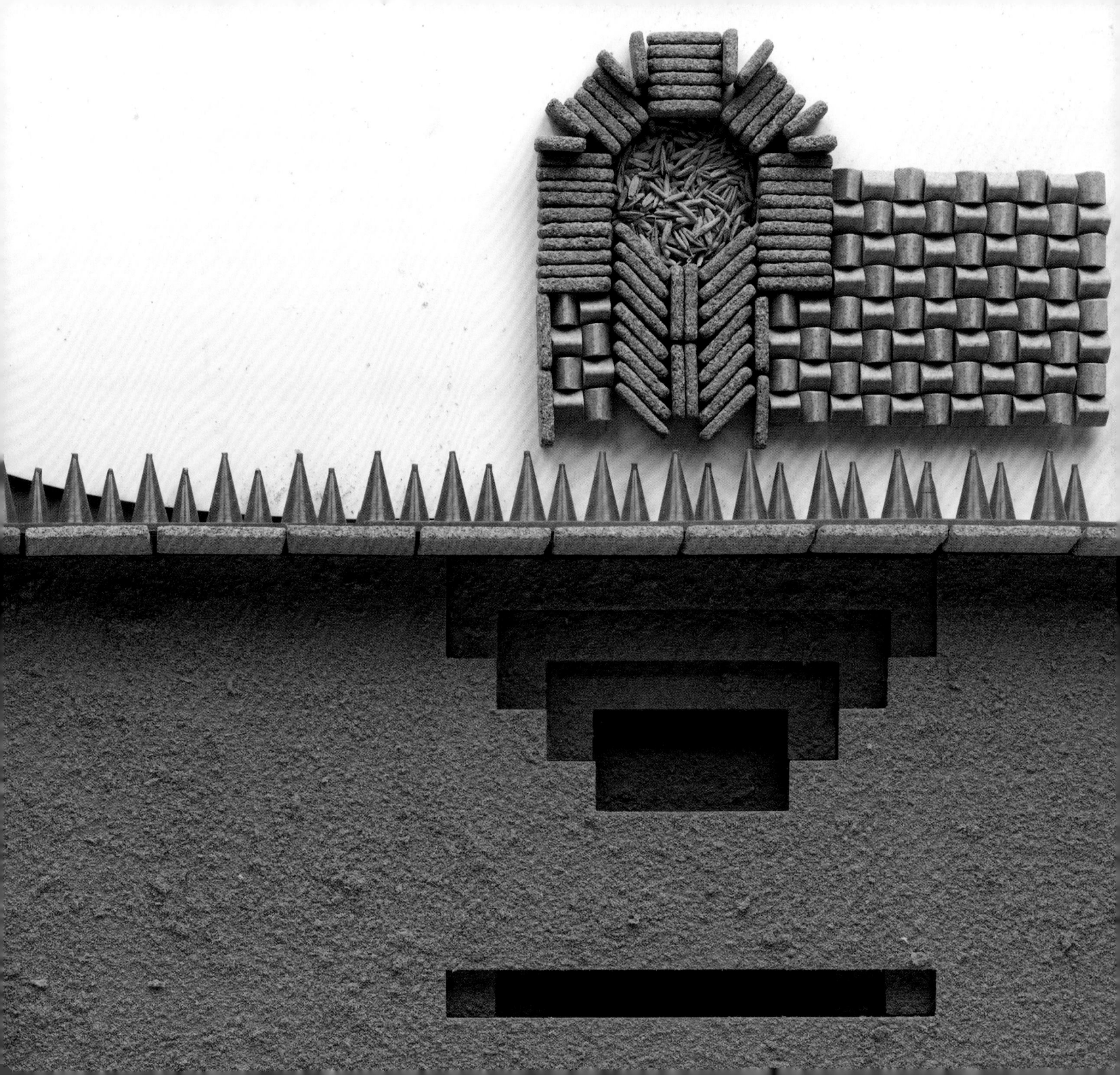

Military

Military architecture both reflected and influenced the course of warfare to a surprising degree. The British formal language of defence structures is often rudimentary and crude when compared to the more considered aesthetic of the *Atlantikwall*, designed by German engineers. Historic England commissioned the publication *Nine Thousand Miles of Concrete*, to document the remaining fragments of military infrastructure, in an attempt to record temporary airfields in England, which have been fading from the landscape at an alarming rate. An analysis of Manston Airfield illustrates the complexity and value of the site in the wake of recent development proposals.

    The resourcefulness of the design of the defence structures demonstrates the extent of practical engineering solutions, using for example shingle collected from the beaches and improvised shuttering. The use of concrete in the construction of the pill boxes has resulted in indomitable structures which are more stable than the condition of the retreat of the cliffs upon which they sit, their presence as much a remnant of World War Two, as a reminder of a former coast line.

Satcom II Satellite Ground Listening Station

Balado, Perth and Kinross, UK

When ARCA heard that the Satcom Ground Station was on the market, I hastily booked a tour. The iconic Perth and Kinross-shire landmark nicknamed, 'The Golf Ball' is situated only 30 kilometres north of Edinburgh. Part of the layout of the Ground Station includes the distinctive white fibreglass radome, which houses a large dish antenna, creating a strking form in the nine acre site. The MOD, which is reported to own approximately 374 sites and land covering almost 25,000 hectares in Scotland, sold the site in 2007 and it has recently reappeared on the market for just under one million pounds. As a large land owner the MOD has recently sold off some striking sites.

The collection of buildings here makes a restrained assemblage, occupying the flat landscape. The buildings are on one-level leading the current owner to pitch it as an ideal home for the elderly. But the striking architecture of the Radar Dome communicates a more futuristic architecture and with that a more dynamic use. Its form retrogressively futuristic, has been designed as a lightweight structure in order for the radar to move around unhindered by any load bearing elements, but its mimicry of a crystalised form formally suggests an architecture of biomimicry or of the architect of the geodesic dome, Buckminster Fuller.

↙
The fibre glass panels on the radome have now become discoloured due to unstable UV filters.

Located in Balado, probably better known to a generation of young Scots as the venue for the 'T-in-the-Park' music festivals, the prime development land or commercial opportunity was previously the location for RAF Balado Bridge, a World War Two airfield. The Radome which conceals the rotating large dish antenna is linked to the main equipment building by a corridor and doors built with enough concrete to withstand a nuclear, biological or chemical attack. An additional accommodation block houses the station mess, recreation and office facilities. Balado was opened by Princess Anne in 1985 and its main purpose was to act as a NATO Intercontinental Ballistic Missile early warning radar.

The satellite communications system in Balado enabled long-distance secure broadcasts between NATO forces using the NATO IV satellite system. This function was also an integral element of the US Air Force's Defence Satellite Communications System, which provided the means necessary for the effective implementation of worldwide military communications. The NATO IV satellite is the same design as the Ministry of Defence's Skynet IV satellite, the next generation of which is being constructed by Paradigm Secure Communications.

The site, sits on a flat plain with the low sound of traffic from the A7, providing a continuous background hum. The corridor runnng the length of the building takes you through a series of blast doors and NBC sealed sections designed to provide isolation chambers in the event of a nuclear attack. The arms room which was used to store the firing equipment, is still intact. The spectacular space of the Radome can be viewed from its central freestanding staircase which takes you to the top of the dome, where the UV filters in the fibre glass panels have turned to a yellowish white, which give them the air of faded modernism.

Kochi Bunker turned Maritime Museum

Kochi, Kerala, India

The Kochi navy play a significant role in the southern Indian state of Kerala. It has its headquarters in Fort Kochi, Kerala at INS Venduruthy, with a fully operating fleet and gunnery training school and residential quarter. The maritime museum, in which the two former bunkers sit neighbours the former spice 'godowns' the name given to the warehouses built by the Dutch which would literally run down to the sea. The buildings look over the Lakshadweep Sea, opening onto the Arabian Sea, which has a constant stream of maritime activity, watching the pace and scale of the vessels is mesmerising. A medley of boats occupies the shores, one sees the traditional Keralan fishing boats glide by the navy surface ships on regular daily patrol and the larger Chinese dredgers which go up and down spraying clouds of grey silt, clearing the channel to keep the Dubai owned port open. The occasional cruise ship adds to the colourful sea traffic.

The historical landscape of the sea in this area witnessed invasions from the Dutch and Portuguese but also a rich history of cosmopolitanism as it sat on the route of the spice trade and the Asian trade routes to Persia and the Orient. During World War Two the fear of the Japanese troops, who at the time were occupying Burma, making inroads to the port of Kochi, drove the British to build a series of bunkers along the coast line, two of which can be visited in Kochi. Built to store arms and ammunition, they are now known as the Indian Naval and Maritime Museum. Too substantial to demolish the Southern Naval Command decided to turn the bunkers into shelters to store antiquities from the Indian Navy in 2001. The unusual squat form with inclining walls, made of granite rather than the local red stone laterite and the juxtaposition of stone walls with the protruding geometrical balconies look as if the engineers were intent of building something of refinement. The balconies were intended for ventilation in the stifling southern Indian summers.

One bunker has been used to narrate the history of Kerala and the other, of the Indian Navy's history. The Maritime Museum in Kochi is India's ode to the glorious past of its majestic Navy. Here we get a glimpse of the formidable sagas, genesis and dealings of one of the top ten naval powers in the world today.

The journey takes you on a special trip that begins from the Indus Valley Civilisation. From there we learn about Kerala's trade links with the Arabs, its famous maritime hero Kunjali Marakkar, the influence of India's maritime power in South East Asia and the Colonisation of the Indian sub-continent by European powers. There is a special section dedicated to post-independence naval victories which include, the Junaghad Operation, the Goa Liberation, Indo-Pak Conflicts of 1965 and 1971, Operation Cactus and the strategic manoeuvres during the Kargil War, the 1999 conflict between India and Pakistan.

→
The bunker's form is a tapering cube with radiused corners and all four elevations are the same dimensions. The rear of the building has climbing steps built into the wall to allow access to the flat roof.

Cold War Military Camp
Sazan Island, Albania

↗ →
The naval officers' rooms looked out on to the Adriatic Sea. The approach to the harbour at Sazan is still equipped with a small Italo-Albanian military base, as holiday makers flood onto the shores on tours around the Albanian coast.

Islands are often shrouded in fantasy, mystery and associations with escapism and isolation. The works of fiction such as R.L. Stevenson's *Treasure Island* (1883) or Arthur Ransom's *Missee Lee* (1941) transport the reader to the possibility of the impossible. Judith Schalanksy, who grew up in East Berlin in the former DDR, wrote the provokingly titled *Atlas of Remote Islands: Fifty Islands I Have Never Set Foot On and Never Will* (2009) which is an exquisite narrative described through rich and imaginative cartographic representations alongside personal interpretations of each island's history, through folklore and fact.

I first came across Sazan, in a newspaper article announcing the island's recent opening after being inaccessible to the public for over a century. Sazan is the largest island in Albania and strategically located between the Strait of Otranto and the entrance to the Bay of Vlorë, forming the border between the Adriatic and Ionian Sea.

Sazan played a crucial part in the defences created by Albania's former Communist leader, Enver Hoxha, who had a paranoid fear of attack, as the only communist country in the Mediterranean. My journey to reach Sazan involved a boat from Corfu port to Saranda and then a five-hour bus journey up the coastline and past a tantalising abandoned former military submarine base, adjacent to the historical site, Porto Palermo, to finally arrive at Vlorë. From here chartered boat tours leave from the central port with permission to land tourists on the site for up to only two hours, to explore the lush island and military ruins. The derelict military base filled with bunkers and tunnels designed to with stand a nuclear attack, opened to tourists in summer 2015. Currently access is limited, with longer term plans by Albania's National Coastal Agency to open it as an eco-tourist destination due to its maritime location which has created a rare ecosystem. The vegetation ranges from Mediterranean to subtropical on account of its warm winters and hot summers,

←
The island supported a small village containing a cinema, grocery store and piazza amongst the terraces. In the background rows of Hoxha's bunkers dot the horizon. It is rumoured that each bunker cost the equivalent of a one bedroom flat.

← ↘
Within the interior of the school desks still occupy the classrooms and the odd abandoned army jacket. The parquet floor is within the entrance foyer of the cinema built within the village layout to entertain the officers and their families.

← In the foreground is the remains of the sculpture commissioned by the local artist from Vlorë with the Military Barracks in the background.

resembling those of the south of Crete, Tunisia and even parts of Egypt. The island was occupied by the Italians who took possession in 1914, renaming it Saseno and established a military command battalion. After World War One, Albania formally ceded the island to Italy as part of the Albano-Italian protocol. The island was part of Italy from 1920 until World War Two, when it was administratively part of the Italian province of Zara. During those years the Italian authorities built a lighthouse and some naval fortifications and populated the island with a few families of fishermen relocated from Apulia. In 1941 it was united to the Italian Governorate of Dalmatia and ceded to Albania in 1947, under the postwar peace treaty with Italy.

During the Cold War, Albania relied heavily on the Soviet Union. In response to the vulnerable position of Albania, surrounded by the perceived threat of invasion, the Soviets built a first-class submarine base and a chemical/biological weapons plant on the island. To support the staff a small village, with a cinema, local shops and school for the officers' children were built with their own electrical generators. Outside the derelict cinema, where the remains of a parquet floor lie in scattered pieces, a sculptural obelisk stands in the foreground against the aqua marine sea. Back on the mainland I meet, by chance, the artist commissioned to design the obelisk in the 1970s who now runs a bookshop but has never been to the island to see its installation. It was rumoured that the officers enjoyed an excellent diet in contrast to the poor conditions for the average Albanian. To this day, Soviet-era gas masks can still be found scattered around the island.

Technically it is still operational as a military base, with a few sailors remaining on the island to offer shelter to navies patrolling Albanian waters. However it is a far cry from the days when more than 3,000 troops were stationed there with enough food, ammunition and fuel to last six months.

Former Radar Station and Bloodhound Missile Base

Bawdsey, Suffolk, UK

Walking, writing and the environment are common bedfellows. The writer and academic W.G. Sebald penned his novel, *The Rings of Saturn*, 1995 whilst walking the 100 miles from Lowestoft to Bungay, along part of the Suffolk coast.

I walk the ridge of higher ground running back from Bawdsey Cliffs, which separates the coast from the low lying land of the Deben Estuary. This shingle beach thins considerably beneath the encased cliff garden of Bawdsey Manor. The manor house was purchased by the RAF in 1936, after the neighbouring military bases at Orfordness were considered inadequate. The estate became the site for two 240ft wooden receiver towers and 360ft steel transmitter towers and Bawdsey became the first Chain Home Radar Station. By the outbreak of World War Two a chain of radar stations was in place around the coast of Britain. RAF Bawdsey was unique in that it had Coast Defence (CD), Chain Home Low (CHL) and Chain Home (CH) equipment together on one site. More usually, CH stations only operated one system and acted as a parent station to those operating the CHL role.

In September 1939, the scientific team was moved from this vulnerable east coast site to Dundee and Bawsdey became an operational rather than a research station. The container in the photograph housed the maintenance material for the Bloodhound missiles. These missiles were poised for launch on the adjacent 'Y' shaped concrete hardstanding from which the six missile launch pads were placed. In May 1990 the Bloodhound force ceased operations and in June all the missiles were withdrawn to RAF West Raynham. Sadly, the last of the giant transmitter masts came down in 2000.

The Bloodhound MKII missile system was a key part of the integrated UK air defences during the Cold War, a British designed defensive weapon to counter nuclear attack with high flying bombers at long range. The missile system was withdrawn from RAF service in 1991, at the end of the Cold War.

Walking this shore line between Shingle Street and Felixstowe, signs of erosion signal its frailties, dropping down to the coast line I spot an incongruous sign issued by the Environmental Agency drawing ones attention to the presence of Betonite mud, stating 'the drilling fluid/mud visible on the beach substrate is an inert clay material'. The narrowest section of beach is groyned with a piled seawall to the foot of the cliff. The beach widens again at the root of the Knolls, at the mouth of the Deben. It is above this point on which the blast container sits, stabilised by steel brackets secured to its concrete base. The elegance of the steel box pinned down by its steel armature conjures up the kinetic possibility of the structure, when once under live testing conditions. Meanwhile on the coast line, the habitats upon the Knolls are mapped and monitored.

The Knolls is the name used to describe the coastal area making up a shingle bank formation extending in parallel to the coast across the entrance to the Deben Estuary. At the entrance to the Deben the northern point is held by a sheet piled wall, backed by a low lying area of shingle deposits. The wall connects through to the Bawdsey Ferry Quay further into the estuary mouth. The area is covered by the sea at high water springs, otherwise this is an intertidal feeding area for birds. The shingle system is very active and includes areas where there is rare habitat, resulting in saline lagoons, being formed and washed away. Here the flora is varied, sea kale, sea vetch, sea pea. On the upper beach, sea couch. The common fauna lists, herring gull, black headed gull, little tern, common tern, scoter, guillemot, cormorant, red breasted merganser. Ringed Plover was previously found on the beach, now departed because of disturbance. Black Redstart was recorded in 2008 as well as common seal, harbour porpoise, herring, cod, whiting, sole, sea trout, sea bass, plaice, turbot, conger, crab, lobster, mussels, shrimps and winkles all are present at the shore line.

Cold War and Military Sites

Roadblock

Narford, Norfolk, UK

The search for the Narford Roadblocks was like looking for needles in haystacks. The rare surviving example of the 'Hairpins' roadblock was built to block a small bridge over the River Nar, in an idyllic river setting in west Norfolk. Sixty years have eroded the steel and minor landslides have toppled the rigid line, so the clarity of the structures as viewed in an original photograph has been disturbed, but nevertheless triumph at finding the structure over a meagre width of River Nar was satisfying. The River Nar is a tributary of the River Great Ouse, which flows through East Anglia before entering the Wash. The 'V' shaped sections of welded steel bar resemble a land art intervention with their regimented rows and strong geometric form.

Two kinds of roadblocks emerged in 1940. One method was simply to put steel poles vertically into dug slots in the road. This was called a 'Hedgehog'. The second was to bend or weld the metal so that it lay at a 60 degree angle and could be slotted into pre-prepared squares dug in the road. These were known as 'Hairpins'. Originally they would have been accompanied by other defences intended to protect the bridge over the river. This defended crossing formed part of the 'Stop Line' that ran from Kings Lynn, Norfolk east across the county to Harleston on the border with Suffolk.

It was well-known to British military planners that the Germans had made extensive use of the road network in France and the Low Countries in order to move their armoured entourage. Therefore Roadblocks were of importance to British anti-invasion strategies and some of those established in 1940 were intended as semi-permanent defences and were made of concrete. These simple roadblocks were formed by obstacles with more sophisticated designs involving large concrete buttresses with sockets across which steel poles could be placed or short sections of railway track. Such defences had the advantage of allowing civilian traffic to use the road whilst the steel rails would be placed to form a barrier only when necessary. The site visit drew me to explore in more detail the meandering River Nar. Its defining feature is its globally rare chalk-stream and has been described as Norfolk's most unspoilt river. As it flows through the downs and fenland of north-west Norfolk, its progression from chalk river to fen river is distinctive as it crosses the diverse range of land topographies. This gives the Nar high conservation value, which is reflected in its Site of Special Scientific Interest (SSSI) designation.

Despite this status its modification along most of its length and pressures on the river are intense. Abstraction, diffuse pollution and the legacy of channel modifications, for example, all inhibit the ecological potential of the river. A programme of river restoration projects on the Nar, with the Norfolk Rivers Trust, identified an exceptionally intact but disconnected river channel. The land bordering this stretch of the Nar, that runs through Emmanuel's Common was historically used as a water meadow for grazing animals. Here, the river had been deepened and straightened to enable drainage of the site, as well as to increase water flows to power the historical Newton Mill.

After studying historic maps and carrying out on-the-ground investigations, the old, disconnected meandering channel was discovered. This channel ran through woodland and remarkably, it had been left unfilled and unchanged since the day it was cut off. Work was undertaken to reconnect the former 600 metre stretch of river with the rest of the Nar by creating a short linking channel upstream and a longer, more natural channel to connect with the main river downstream. Scrub was cleared to open up and improve the flow of water.

This relic channel is a true rarity on English chalk-streams. More or less every metre of every river has been modified for one reason or another. To find 500 metres left more or less as in the Ice-Age was a unique discovery.

↗
The steel sections which are sinking into the soil are now surrounded by woodland plants.

Pillbox in Former Monastic Building

Minsmere Marshes, Suffolk, UK

The Pillbox inserted into the ancient archeological ruin in Minsmere Marshes, near Saxmundham, appears a parasitic intrusion into what has been described as a significant piece of Suffolk's medieval history. However on closer inspection the concrete pillbox provides structural support to prop up the remains of Leiston Chapel, a form of mutualism where a symbiotic relationship between buildings is created. During World War Two Minsmere was one of the key defence sites on the Suffolk Coast, sitting on what was described as the 'coastal crust'. To protect the coast from German forces a management programme of artificial flooding, as a defence measure on what was previously agricultural land was introduced. In June 1940 the sea sluice was opened and the gate allowing the exit of freshwater from the river closed. When the whole area was flooded the sea sluice was closed and the area remained inundated until 1945, when the operation of the sluices returned to normal.

This natural manipulation of the vulnerable coast line has contributed to Minsmere's current success as a Nature Reserve and the perfect habitat for wild birds. The site is home to a unique collection of birds which includes marsh harriers, bitterns and avocets. The coastal area around Suffolk consists of marsh land, managed as heath, through which a series of slow moving watercourses run, finding their way to the sea. This is what is described as marsh and fen. Suffolk was particularly vulnerable to enemy attack because of its proximity to the German occupied ports in the Netherlands and Belgium. After the war the larger fortifications were dealt with on site. At Dunwich, for example, a Suffolk Square pillbox is known to remain beneath the beach in the spot where it was pushed into a hole, excavated solely for the purpose of burying it. Early post-war illustrations depict life slowly getting back to normal, albeit against the backdrop of the remnants of the 'coastal crust'. Away from holiday resorts the removal of the former defences was more

Cold War and Military Sites

← The insertion of the pillbox into the ancient lime mortar and flint walls of the abbey makes a remarkable marrying of the military inserted into the religious.

→ The concrete infill into the brick arch demonstrates a sophisticated use of brick although it is not certain if it was a later addition to the original 12th century construction.

piecemeal. Dunwich Heath was acquired by the National Trust and here a heath fire, during the 1960s exploded so much ordnance, that the area was systematically cleared. Manpower from Eastern Europe, as part of the post-war resettlement programme was also introduced to remove most of the concrete defences on the heath and beach.

Sitting on the hillock above the Minsmere marshland is the former monastic building. Research led by Suffolk County Council's Archaeological Conservation Team confirmed that the chapel is situated in the centre of what was originally a Premonstratensian Abbey, an order of canons founded in France in 1102. The conservation of Leiston Chapel has given archaeologists a valuable insight into how the land was used dating back to 1182. Leiston Abbey, formerly known as St Mary's Abbey, was founded in 1182 near Minsmere, by Ranulf de Glanville, Lord Chief Justice to King Henry II. Fearing an increased risk of flooding, the monks abandoned the abbey in 1363 and a new complex was built four kilometres further inland by Robert de Ufford, Earl of Suffolk. Documentary evidence suggests that a presence was maintained on the original site until the dissolution in 1537 and Leiston Chapel is the only surviving evidence of this continuing occupation. John Ette, ancient monuments inspector for Historic England in the east region, confirmed its status, "This is of great archaeological importance, being the early site of the Leiston Abbey and where the monks created their community before they were inundated by coastal processes. The concrete pillbox and machine gun emplacement were inserted into the eastern end of the structure. At the highest point in the landscape and with a building already offering the potential for camouflage, the hillock was an obvious site for a strong point." The medieval walls of the chapel act as a shell for the rectangular concrete pillbox that was built within the structure and provided with numerous firing points for infantry men.

Gun Battery

Abbot's Cliff, Kent, UK

If you walk along the North Downs Way, the long-distance path which stretches along the Dover Cliffs, a series of World War Two Batteries will come into view. The Abbot's Cliff Gun Battery was part of the coastal defence system built in 1941 between Dover and Folkestone in southeast England. It is on the cliff-edge between Abbot's Cliff and Shakespeare Cliff. Separated from France by only 34 kilometres of sea, Kent has often been threatened by invasion. During World War Two, new anti-invasion defences were built, such as those at Hougham between Dover and Folkestone and earlier ones were re-armed. Cross-Channel guns, two of them nicknamed 'Winnie' and 'Pooh', were positioned on the cliffs at St Margaret's near Dover as a response to the danger from German long-range guns in the Pas-de-Calais. The Batteries to the east and west of Dover were designated as a fortress and each one had an underground plotting room from where the guns could be controlled. The Hougham Battery further down the coastal way towards Dover has been partially covered with earth so little can be seen of the structure since the construction of the A20 in the 1970s. Access is still possible to the underground battery plotting room.

The cuboid form of Abbot's Cliff Battery is rare with no other archived examples of similar form I know of. The simplicity of the structure's geometry, suggests the language of a pavilion, rather than a defensive structure. The walls show the clear lines of each concrete pour with the large percentage of aggregate to sand in the concrete mix, giving the appearance of a pebble beach standing vertically to the ground. Lichens have grown inside the structure, similar to those which grow on rocks and stones. The healthy lichens are detectable by the strong growth in the centre. In the classic definition of lichenology, the lichen grows from the edges therefore if the centres begin to die this is indicative of the state of the whole lichen. Any attempt to photograph the building's front elevation would be fool hardy as the cliff shows significant signs of erosion.

The name Abbot's Cliff also describes the large holiday home near Folkestone, with a little known wartime history. A group of special duties linguists, were employed to intercept signals from German traffic, mainly German Naval Traffic. Abbot's Cliff was one of 18 listening posts, called Y Stations, based around the Southeast coast. Overlooking the English Channel, this was one of the busiest and most important monitoring stations.

One of the operators, Pam Torrens, was asked during a BBC documentary to revisit the house and recalls the techniques they used, "We sat at radio sets which had a dial on them and we travelled from one end of the 20 megahits to the other and then we went back again, and we investigated any signal we came across. You had to keep twiddling, so we were called 'twiddlers'… You'd go back and forth and if you found a signal." The women were chosen because they could speak fluent German, but had to learn German naval terms, code names and additional secret codes.

→
Abbot's Cliff is an example of an anti-invasion defence built between Dover and Folkestone.

Atlantic Wall

Sheriff Muir, Stirlingshire, UK

It was a bitter January day when I eventually located the remnants of the reinforced concrete mock-up of the anti-invasion Atlantic Wall. Against the grey sky the hostile land, which sits at a height 292 metres, five kilometres east of Dunblane, on the north-west fringes of the Ochils, has few redeeming features. The land is mainly given over to forestry with seasonal grouse shooting and sheep grazing. An isolated inn sits a few kilometres down the Sherriffmuir Road, an optimistic siting, in its hope for passing trade.

Following the Nazi's occupation of Europe, Hitler ordered the construction of a massive series of defences along Europe's coastline, often using POW labour. The key element of these was the infamous Atlantic Wall, designed to repel tanks. They were constructed from reinforced concrete, at which the Germans excelled. In 1943, in order to determine how to breach these walls the British formed the Anti-Concrete Committee. The plans for the Atlantic Wall were reportedly smuggled out of occupied Europe in a biscuit tin courtesy of a French painter and decorator called Rene Duchez. Duchez got his hands on the blueprints for the German defences while painting the offices of the engineering group TODT, which had been hired to build the Wall. In order to work out how to breach these defences the British constructed a series of replicas across Britain and the biggest and best preserved of these is at Sheriffmuir, near Stirling. Sheriffmuir was chosen for both its relative isolation and its proximity to the major transport hub at Stirling. There is another example at Hankley Common, Surrey.

A short walk from the road, the wall stands 86 metres in length from north-east to south-west and about three metres in height. Just over half of the length of the wall is three metres thick, stepping down to 0.7 metres at the south-west end, where the wall curves round slightly to the west. The rear face of the wall is vertical for about half its height, sloping inwards towards the top, which is flat. The front, or seaward side slopes outwards to create an overhang, with a small inward slope at the top along which there are iron pickets to carry barbed wire. The corrugations of the shuttering used in the construction of the wall are clearly visible, as are individual mounds of concrete. Some care has been taken in finishing off the surfaces where the initial dumping of concrete has left gaps. A tunnel, 0.6 metres wide, runs through the wall about half way along. The front face is extensively pitted by impacts from weapons of a variety of calibres revealing the reinforcement rods, but the most spectacular damage is a four metre wide breach in the wall from which a spread of debris extends some 40 metres away. The wall is fronted by a flat-bottomed anti-tank ditch. A trench lying 30 metres to the north-west of the wall may have connected a network of trenches with a bunker.

This bunker incorporates a Tobruk shelter consisting of a sunken chamber with two observation and firing holes in the roof. Initially developed by the Italian Army in North Africa, these were quickly adopted by the Afrika Korps and were used by the German Army as an integral part of many Atlantic Wall defences. The Torbruk shelter, is based on the German tactic of burying tanks in sand, leaving only their main gun barrel exposed. The shelter develops this idea into two fixed gun positions and an underground shelter. To the east of the bunker is a large disturbed hollow full of ironwork which extends as far as a grass-covered, concrete bunker, which may have been octagonal in plan. This top-secret research and training ground was used in the preparation for D-Day. The complex of reconstructions reflects both German offensive and defensive positions and recreates the ground conditions and distances from the landing craft in the sea, all the way to the wall.

Langham Dome

Neatshead, Norfolk, UK

On approaching the site the scattering of picnic benches politely arranged around the concrete and steel hemispherical dome give the building a suburban air. Sitting in a wider landscape of fields, the Dome was put on the Historic England annual 'at risk' register. After a local campaign by Langham Parish Council, it has been successfully restored as a museum.

The Dome Trainer (1963) is constructed of steel with a concrete outer layer. Dating back to 1943 it is one of about 40 originally built and of only a handful to survive. The dome was a training aid, a type of early flight simulator for ground-to-air gunnery. Projection equipment inside the structure played film of aircraft making mock attacks moving around the interior via cameras and mirrors, accompanied by realistic sound.

The servicemen sat at a mock anti-aircraft gun and had to shoot at the simulated enemy aircraft, while an instructor would measure the accuracy of the shooter projected onto the interior. Once gunners became proficient, they moved onto real targets being towed by aircraft on the North Norfolk coast.

The Dome sits in what was formerly Langham Airfield which has an impressive history. Established in 1940 as an emergency landing ground, it soon became a satellite station for the larger RAF Bircham Newton and was home to one of the RAF's Coastal Command Strike Wings, tasked with striking against German shipping. By 1942 it was a station in its own right and housed Fairy Swordfish bi-planes, a type of Torpedo bomber introduced in 1936. For a time it also acted as a station for air sea rescue.

The airfield was upgraded In 1943 and a year later was re-opened and operated Bristol Beaufighters primarily flying missions against German shipping. After the war, Langham became a centre for meteorological flying and a training station for the Dutch Technical School, but was gradually wound down and sold off in 1961 to Bernard Matthews, for the less illustrious activity of turkey rearing.

The cut in the ground provides a stepped route to the underground shelter. Access to the shelter is open and to the rear of this is the ground bunker which can be explored.

→
The picnic benches sitting on the maintained lawn fan out from the dome's circular footprint. The museum is open to the public.

The Control Tower is now a prime spot to watch the weather providing views across the channel in the direction of Ramsgate.

Manston Airfield

Manston, Kent, UK

I recorded the now decommissioned Kent International Airport, or Manston Airfield as it was first named, after reviewing the site for a planning application to develop the area into a satellite village. The predictable and vanilla proposal resolved to leave the runway intact, save for a few diagonal incisions to create footpaths, breaking the clarity of the runway's horizontal plane. The decision was driven primarily to avoid the immense cost of disposing of the sheer quantity of tarmac and concrete substrate. There were no creative proposals for how the acres of hardstanding might create engaging programmes, be it ecological or agricultural. Former airfields in Germany have been turned into landscape parks by breaking up the surface of the tarmac to allow indigenous planting to take seed, such as the former US army helicopter airfield Alter Flugplatz Kalbach, near Frankfurt-am-Main.

The airport lies ten kilometres west of Ramsgate, in the district of Thanet. The three kilometre runway; too costly to dig up, sits on a substrate of approximately one metre. As on-going proposals for its future are debated, it seems timely to ask how future designs might deal with the sheer quantity of tarmac and bitumen. How can the material nature, the bitumous carbonated oil, of the runway be considered in future designs. Here I am reminded of the American land artist, Robert Smithson's writing and land art pieces such as *Asphalt Rundown*, (1968). Or an earlier work, *Tar Pool and Gravel Pit* (1966), described by Smithson, "A molten substance is poured into a square sink that

↗
The runway was built in two sections firstly as the World War One RAF base and secondly expanded during World War Two.

→ ↘
The terminal waiting room with its red carpet which gives the space a rose tint would provide passengers with an airside view of the planes. The linoleum inlay of the globe greets passengers in the main terminal building.

is surrounded by another square sink of coarse gravel. The tar cools and flattens into a sticky level deposit. This carbonaceous sediment brings to mind a tertiary world of petroleum, asphalts, ozocerite, and bituminous agglomerations." Bringing together the industrialised material poured into the worked over and mined land, Smithson is making a connection between the composition of the material and its geological makeup.

Manston started its aviation days as a Royal Naval Station in 1916, with a base at Westgate Bay, near Deal, for seaplanes. By 1917, Manston airfield had grown to include four underground hangars, its own railway line to Birchington, a power station to generate electricity, barracks for 3,000 men and even an indoor swimming pool.

The first jet fighters arrived at Manston, to attack the flying bombs, (1944's version of the cruise missile), during the Battle of Britain. The site boasted the longest and widest runway in southern England, built to allow badly damaged aircraft returning from Europe to a safe haven, with the 'Fido Fog' dispersal system, made up of burning lines of petroleum, to facilitate landings in any weather. In 1960 Manston returned to the RAF as a major diversionary airfield for aircraft in trouble. The fire school was formed to train RAF firemen in everything from aircraft fires to rescuing car crash victims. In 1998 the MOD sold RAF Manston and civil aviation companies arrived, taking 700,000 people on their first foreign holiday in one year. Manston's illustrious history is now confined to two flight museums on site, the *Spitfire and Hurricane Museum* and the *RAF Manston History Museum* stuffed full of war memorabilia which attracts local residents and flight enthusiasts.

Recent controversy over the airfield's future is stalling its redevelopment. In 2014, the operating airport was sold to Ann Gloag of Stagecoach, for a nominal fee of one pound, on the premise that it would continue to operate as a commercial airport. At this point the idea was mooted that it might be a contender as a viable alternative to building a controversial new runway in the Thames estuary. Stagecoach quickly realised the improbability of its survival as a viable business. Competition from low cost airlines concentrated around the major airports meant that flights dwindled to barely a few KLM flights a week and intermittent cargo planes bringing tropical fruit. This extravagant cargo became redundant when the hydroponic farm, *Thanet Earth* opened in 2008, a few kilometres from the airfield, outside Margate. During its heyday the airfield's colourful history, as told in the local press, included the "bizarre sight of the Airbus 300-600 Tehran-bound plane which became a regular event as it refueled at one of the UK's smallest airports, so the scheduled flight can return to Iran." Banned from filling up at Heathrow because of Western-imposed sanctions, the plane with up to 266 passengers would make the quick hop to the virtually deserted but privately-owned airfield to refuel.

At the present time, on approaching Manston Airport one is met at the entrance with the shed like construction of the former Passenger Terminal. The scale of the building is modest, built to accommodate the predicted one million passengers per year, in reality it was barely over 50,000 passengers during normal operation. The floor of the departure hall is covered with a linoleum map of the world, signaling the airport's global aspirations. A steel frame with in-fill panels of dubious lightweight material, shreds strands of fibre onto the departure lounge. The runway in contrast to the ancillary buildings could be described as a gigantic carpet which spreads its matt surface, over three hectares of the site. Currently striped with white paint markings to define the channels for rows of lorries, in anticipation of *Operation Stack*, the predicted backlogs of lorry cargo due to the migrant crisis at Calais and more recently in the light of Brexit uncertainties.

↗
The runway was recently allocated as a parking area for 'Operation Stack' a measure to counteract the potential backlog of trucks held up at the Dover/Calais crossing.

Bombing Decoy

Wormegay, West Norfolk, UK

↙
The remains of the decoy structure stands in a field of grazing cattle. The platform with the scaffolding balcony creates an impression of a drawn line against the sky.

The isolated marshland around Wormegay in west Norfolk is the site of a decoy airfield, built to draw German bombers away from genuine targets. The decoy had mock flare paths and runway lights to confuse enemy bombers at night and distract them from the parent airfield, in this case RAF Marham.

To reach the site at Wormegay, you cross a field of grazing cattle and a few fences to find the cluster of single storey buildings which makes up a collaged group of forms and materials. The surviving building is a 'Combined Field Control Room' and 'Generator House', which was able to simulate a false airfield. The remains of the building consists of a crew shelter and the generator building, with the ruins of a blast wall at the entrance. Originally, at least part of this building would have been covered with earth, since removed.

Wormegay was a 'Q' site, designated for night-time operations and involved the creation of a false airfield runway. 'Q' Sites were also given a form of searchlight, known as a 'Scarecrow' that gave the impression that aircraft were taking off. During World War Two a secret department was formed at Britain's Air Ministry to co-ordinate a strategy to defeat German bombing by deception. With the help of leading technicians from the film industry, a broad range of day and night decoy sites were built throughout the island, to mislead enemy bombers.

The decoy site programme began in January 1940 and developed into a complex deception strategy, using four main methods: day and night dummy aerodromes ('K' and 'Q' sites); diversionary fires ('QF' sites and 'Starfish'); simulated urban lighting ('QL' sites); and dummy factories and buildings. Urban decoy fires were known as 'SF', 'Special Fires' and Starfish, to distinguish them from the smaller 'QF' installations. These were the most technically sophisticated of all the types, with each Starfish replicating the fire effects an enemy aircrew would expect to see when their target had been successfully set alight.

This campaign of illusion was masterminded by an engineer and retired Air Ministry officer, Colonel John Fisher Turner. Colonel Turner formed a team with the best film studio tradesmen, carpenters and engineers, all for the construction of an elaborate network of dummy airfields and hundreds of decoy sites. These sites were set up in large areas of open space to protect the genuine sites they were imitating which could be towns, military bases, factories, airfields or railway marshalling yards or docks.

Tanks containing paraffin or diesel were placed on top of six metre towers, arranged to resemble rows of buildings or industrial complexes. A valve that operated like a toilet flush was opened to release the fuel on to burning coal, creating an instant blaze and engulfing the area in black smoke. Then the fire was flushed with water to send a column of steam into the night sky. It is believed that there were around 230 dummy airfields in the UK and 400 dummy urban and industrial sites although very few of any of these decoys, now survive, most having been cleared after the war.

Due to the heavy bombing to which several areas were exposed, the risk of encountering Unexploded Ordnance (UXO) becomes an important factor in contemporary construction projects and new developments. The company *Ground Source* saw this opportunity to offer access to geo-referenced unexploded ordnance throughout the UK to developers. The analysis examines thousands of sites to mitigate bomb risk tracking previous bomb excavations and accurate bomb density mapping based on hundreds of datasets.

Casabianca Battery

Lido di Venezia, Italy

The Lido is approximately 11 kilometres long and is a sand bank forming a natural barrier between the lagoon and the sea. At the end of the eighteenth century, the island was gifted by the Republic of Venice to the people of Armenia.

Historically settlements began in the centre of the island, known as Malamocco, which served as an ancient port. Records show that in 1202 thousands of Crusaders used the Lido as a camp, detained there as they could not pay their passage to Venice. The main developments took place in the nineteenth century with the opening of exclusive resorts attracting writers and film stars and in 1932 the film festival was established, located on the northern part of the island. In 1908 the Lido was chosen as a site to build a 'Garden City' designed by Duilio Torres. This drew in the middle-class families from Venice who built villas both in the Art Nouveau style and neo-Romano-Byzantine style.

In 1909 it became a centre for aviation, with the lagoon providing an ideal site for hydroplanes and in 1934, the first civil air terminal in Italy which featured a modernist building by Felice Santabarbara and Mario Emmer.

←
The concrete bunker is one of the many buildings scattered on the site, in the stretch along the Lido's linear land mass.

↗
The grandeur of the earlier nineteenth century battery with its dressed stone and Renaissance style arches contrasts with the wooden shuttered concrete bunker built as a rapid response to World War Two.

From the 1950s the Lido's attraction as a holiday site began to wane with 300 bed hotels such as the *Excelsior* looking tired and dilapidated. Renata Codello, the Italian government's architecture and environment officer for Venice and the Lagoon, described the Lido as "ghostly and sad, frozen in time". But recent investments in the classic hotels and the problem of overcrowding in Venice itself has renewed the island's popularity. Apart from the hotels, Codello has catalogued 150 exceptional examples of Art Nouveau and Art Deco villas on the Lido, giving it Italy's largest concentration of architecture from that era.

A few kilometres south of the main town, on the outskirts of Malamocco stands the nineteenth century battery, Casabianca, which belonged to the complex defensive system built to defend the city of Venice. Its original structure dates back to the second Austrian rule. In the 1880s Italians extended and strengthened it. Between 1909 and 1913 away from the seaward elevation the defensive coast battery Angelo Emo was built, using in-situ concrete.

The contrast of the twentieth century additions to the brick arched interior blockhouse from the earlier period is striking with the two styles crashing into one another. The building is owned by the Military property state department and is in a run-down state. Access is prohibited and the residential neighbours do not welcome inquisitive visitors. Further down the coast there is the abandoned children's holiday camp 'Principi di Piemonte Camp' at Alberoni (1936–37) which is a rigorous piece of Italian rationalist architecture and houses a ramp to accommodate the 600 children exiting from the dormitory, a veritable example of an 'architectural promenade'. The architect of the scheme, Daniele Calabi (1906–64), was heavily influenced by the French architect Marcel Lods (1891–1978) who built the first example of a prefabricated residential complex, the 'Cite du Champ des Oiseaux' in Bayeux in 1931.

Favignana Bunker

Aegadian Islands, Sicily

The Aegadian Islands are situated in the Mediterranean, 15 kilometres from the most westerly point of Sicily. The archipelago is made up of three small mountainous islands, Favignana, Levano and Marettimo and some minor rocky outcrops. The Bunker sits just outside the bay of the port town Favignana, which is dominated by a now disused but resplendent, tuna fishing factory, the Tonnara di Favigana. This is a testament to the 'mattanza' the annual tuna cull, which until 2007, took place every year during May and June, turning the sea blood red. The beauty of the islands was described in the Odyssey (Book IX), when Homer´s Ulysses arrives in what he describes as the 'Island of Goats'. Historians claim that the first inhabitants of Sicily were the Feaci (sailors) and the Lestrigoni (farmers) who came from Epiro (Epirus). They originally inhabited the cave structures from the first century BC, where even today, traces of cave paintings are visible in the Grotta del Pozza, a cave which was discovered in 1968, lying underneath a cemetery. The slivers of oxidised and fragmented bones found in Favignana show signs of the diet of a small human settlement which lived by the sea, nourished by fish and molluscs. By living in the caves they were able to take on a sedentary lifestyle and develop craftsmanship and art.

The island has been the victim of many historical battles, for example the Punic Wars when the spoils of the Roman victory included Favignana, which provided the Roman Empire with a rich source of rock made of volcanic ash called tuff stone. Quarries were dug all over the island and these angular depressions are very much part of the topographical make-up of Favignana today. During this period the islands were frequently plundered coinciding with the Carthaginian trade and military power at the height of its glory, when it was incorporated, in a sole dominion, of North Africa and West Sicily.

During World War Two the Italian dictator Mussolini, who led his country to war allied with the Germans, identified the strategic strength of this small cluster of islands and of Sicily itself. The war left a legacy of bunkers built to protect the major ports both on Sicily and scattered around the Aegadian Islands.

As one approaches the bay of Favignana by sea, the World War Two Bunker comes into view. Leading up from the sea edge is a series of steps worn into the porous stone, probably created long before the Bunker's arrival, suggesting the approach is one favoured by fisherman over the years.

The Bunker has taken on an almost magical appearance with the structure's eroded concrete and the irregularly protruding edges, resembling the wings of Icarus rather than the chill of war. The site is on the north side of the island, where the strongest winds are directed. The Mistral winds from the north-west, also hit the northern coast as winter turns to spring, causing higher and more aggressive tidal erosion.

The historical interest and archaeological profile of the Archipelago lies not in the classical ancient ruins but in the high number of caves excavated by sea erosion in the limestone cliffs of Favignana and Levanzo during Pleistocene, the last Ice Age, whereas Marettimo, the smallest island in the trio, due to its different geo-lithological conformation has fewer under water caves but dramatic rocky outcrops and bays.

In the background the chimney of the Tuna Factory can be seen with the pitched roofs.

Cold War and Military Sites

← ↗
The Bunker sits in the outskirts of Favignana town surrounded by volcanic rock. The steps down to the sea have been carved out and worn away by the tides.

Cold War and Military Sites

Modern Follies and Religious Buildings

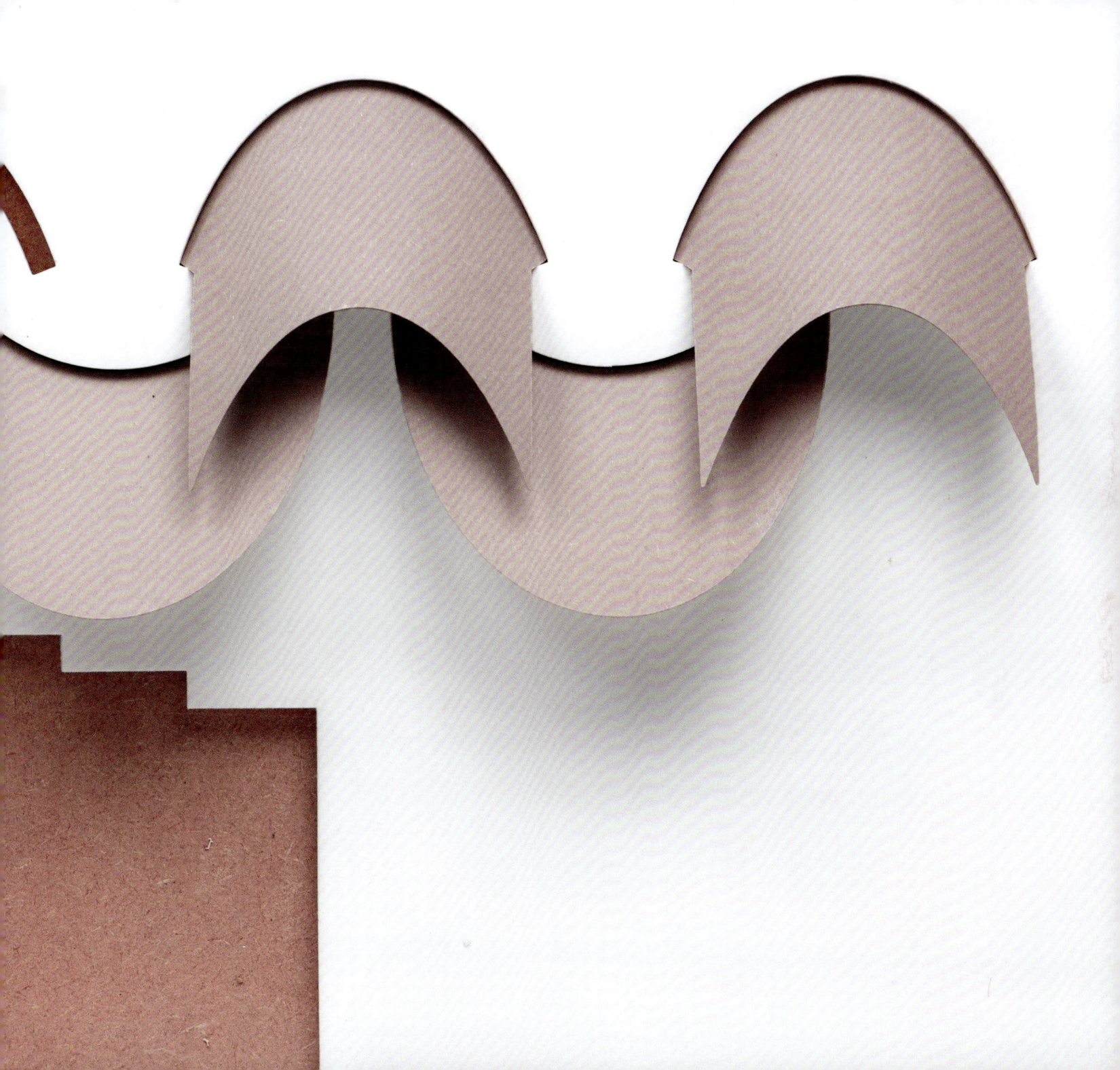

Follies & Religious

The architecture of the folly suggests a whimsical structure. Follies became fashionable in the eighteenth century bejewelling large swathes of the English Landscape. William Kent, who introduced the concept of 'natural landscape', designed a Hermitage in Richmond Gardens which became a popular building type in English Gardens alongside grottos and caves. Although not to everyone's taste as a local writer described the Hermitage as, 'very Grotesque and representing rude Nature.'

    If there is a contemporary version of the folly, or hermitage it is reflected in the commissioning of outdoor sculptural structures, or pavilions of which there has been a recent explosion. La Stella in Sicily, both public art piece and gateway, was commissioned to create an identity for the new town, Gibellina Nuova, built to rehouse the nearby earthquake victims. In the case of the Crystal Palace Pavilion, from a distance the structure reads as purely sculptural but on approaching hints at its architectural purpose become clearer. Its bold use of Corten steel is a perfect antidote to the park setting, created for the relocated Great Exhibition building.

La Stella

Gibellina Nuova, Sicily

I went in search of the landscape installation, *Grande Cretto di Gibellina* Antico 20 kilometres from Trapani in Sicily. The Italian artist Alberto Burri, a member of the *Arte Povera* movement, was one of a group of invited artists to respond to the complete destruction of the town, Gibellina after it was flattened by an earthquake in 1968. Instead of rebuilding the old town it was decided that a new Gibillina would be created driven by a utopian programme of public art and bold new structures, named Gibellina Nuova, 11 kilometres from the old centre. Deeply moved by the effect of the earthquake, Burri was intent not to build within the new town and instead offered to cover the rubble of the destroyed site, which currently still lies in ruins, with the pouring of an immense structure covered in white cement. Lack of funds drove the local mayor, a supporter of Burri's work to ask for the help of the military to move the rubble and enclose it in metal nets, with the assistance of the contractors enlisted in building Gibellina Nuova.

    Burri's project began in 1985 but by 1989 the work was stopped, leaving nearly a third of the total surface area incomplete. In 2015 to mark the one hundredth anniversary of Burri, the structure *Grande Cretto* was completed. The scale of the work is immense, probably one of largest pieces of landscape art in Europe, covering approximately 85,000 sq metres. Aerial view footage shows a solid mass of white stone with paths cast into it to mark the old street patterns, like an alien rock formation. The smooth cement covers the enclosed remnants of the town. I came very close, on my pilgrimage to visit one of Arte Povera's most recognised works amongst the art world cognoscenti, but wasn't aware that it was outside of

←
The stainless steel sculpture greets you on the main entrance to Gibellina Nuova. The piece is one of the 100 hundred outdoor sculptures.

the actual town, Gibellina Nuova, as its location is merely cited as Gibellina, with no distinction between Antico and Nuova. On asking for directions, in what is a ghost town singed by the southern Italian heat, heads just shook. There were no taxis or buses and I had arrived by train of which there were very few. I had to make do with Gibellina Nuova, which suffered all the mistakes of new town architecture, low-density planning with little cultural infrastructure. Built to house the displaced residents, around a series of well-meaning civic ideas, the soul of the old town was lost and residents moved away leaving the ongoing project in a state of incompletion. Aside from the lack of funding for the installations and upkeep of the buildings an underlying and more crippling problem emerged. Although some local artisans and craftsmen participated in the process, many victims, thrust into a new environment of wide boulevards and isolated works of art in which they had no stake, felt disoriented. "Sometimes the elders seemed lost in a metaphysical town ill-suited to their needs and habits," says Cuschera one of the invited artists.

The wide streets and lack of intimate public spaces means that the town has a lifeless air. Dotted with bold public art pieces as part of the experimental programme, they have no audience to celebrate their claim to space. Built to accommodate 100,000 residents there are currently barely 6,000 living in the town.

On arriving at the entrance to Gibellina, the 26 metre stainless steel sculpture, *La Stella* by Pietro Consagra greets you, straddling over both lanes of the dual carriage way. Consagra was also invited to design the gates to the cemetery of Gibellina Nuova in which the earthquake victims were laid to rest. *La Stella* rises above the whole of the Belice valley. As you move through the town more sculptures reveal themselves, as if one is walking through an open air sculpture park. More than 76 Brutalist, Postmodern and more contemporary buildings and monuments were begun over five decades, many from elements that had survived the earthquake. The artist Nanda Vigo, who repurposed a fountain, an arch and some pillars from the old town for her 1976 installations *Tracce Antropomorfe*, says, "everybody was free to choose location and materials. There were no restrictions. The only problem was the money, which of course was not there." The Mayor Ludovico Corrao scraped together funding for some projects, but many of the works were ultimately donated by the artists. The experiment to use the town as a test bed for integrating art has seen a revisiting of interest with Alessandro La Grassa, president of the Centre for Social and Economic Research of Southern Italy announcing its role as an Art Town. The proposed plans were presented at the Venice Architectural Biennale in 2018 and the next chapter for the town may have a more optimistic future.

→
Gibellina is located in the middle of Sicily between two great monuments of the past Segesta and Selinunte.

Modern Follies and Religious Buildings

Spanish Chapel
Iznájar, Cordoba Province, Spain

↗
The grilled window has the delicate detail of the cross. A tradition of local blacksmith workshops can still be found in the small towns in the south of Spain.

Winding down to Lake Iznájar, the terrain changes from continuous rows of olive trees with terraces cut into sharply angled slopes, to densely planted pines. An old enameled road sign points in the direction of Granada, Cordoba, Malaga, although there appear to be virtually no passing cars, except the odd fisherman on his way to the lakeside.

The Chapel sits amongst the pines near the lake which crosses the three provinces in Andalucia. It has a single pitch roof with a series of punched windows in the side elevation filled with glass bricks, the contemporary equivalent of a clerestory. The lower windows are fitted with iron bars so beloved of the Spanish. These have the detail of a welded cross on top of the grating, made of the same bar thickness.

The four columns which support a covered overhang for the congregation to linger outside the front entrance, sweeps back in a single pitch to meet the bell tower which, in contrast to the pantiled roof is rendered in plaster with a steel cross. The front façade is clad with a veneer of crazy paving stones lending it an era of the 70s. In the foreground of the Chapel, is a large landscaped area with benches of the same period. The mature garden has been planted with bougainvillea and pines.

The Chapel is derelict and boarded up. It was probably used to service the communities around the dam or as part of a holiday village for a religious denomination, as it neighbours a complex of single storey residential units, which face onto the overgrown area equipped with public seating.

→
The quadrilateral windows with circular glass bricks on the side elevation following the pitch of the ceiling suggest the stepping up to the altar, a form of clerestory.

Modern Follies and Religious Buildings

↘
The now boarded up front entrance has been prized apart to strip the building of any fittings. The structure is relatively economical with the precast exposed concrete beams.

Crystal Palace Concert Pavilion

Crystal Palace Park, London, UK

The concert platform in Crystal Palace Park, south London is a striking piece of sculpture. Its simple rectangular form is composed of a surging cantilevered canopy which seers towards the sky, while the strong geometric lines create a dramatic figure against the backdrop of the park. It sits in a lake, which adds to the drama of the structure. The classic architectural figure ground relationship is boldly executed.

    The competition to design a permanent concert platform was won in 1996, by the London based practice Ian Ritchie Architects. The pavilion is situated within a large bowl shape in the Joseph Paxton designed landscape which was completed in 1864. The new intervention is capable of seating 8,000 people and when functioning had the first outdoor active acoustic system.

← The two sentinel posts which stand at either side of the platform discreetly house the sophisticated acoustic system.

↗ The oak and steel platform, which was designed to be economic and resistant to vandalism, unfortunately has not been maintained.

↙
The self-weathering Corten steel creates its own patina thus becoming sculptural but not sculpture in the architect's words.

Ian Ritchie's design concept embodied three principles; to situate the structure within a reading of the landscape context which led to the use of Corten steel, a desire for the structure's mass to be perceived as having weight to provide a sense of permanence, and an approach that aims to embed it within its natural environment. In practical terms, the pavilion is robust, resistant to vandalism, economic and requires very low maintenance. To enter the interior a draw bridge door drops down from the underside of the cantilevered stage overhang. Its outer surface is made entirely of deep red oxidised Corten. Externally the steel and oak stage provides a warm counterpoint to the park's mature trees and internally the design palette introduces more industrial materials such as silver 'aluzinc' panels and a blue floor.

 The building's life span is threatened by a lack of funding to cover its maintenance but applications for future funding might see the building resurrected as part of a wider regeneration plan for the park which has recently overseen the restoration of the beloved 'Dinosaur Park' originally opened in 1853 and recently given a Grade 1 listing. But currently it stands in danger of slowly turning into a ruin. The lack of programming for the building is reflected in its abandoned state. The oak platform of the outdoor stage is rotting. The structure with its potential to perform an engaging role with the public providing a performance venue in the open air is under threat both from the weather and lack of financial support. Its stage is now circumnavigated by a few mallard ducks who battle through the moat covered in blanket weed.

St Paul's Church

Glenrothes, Fife, UK

The architectural practice, Gillespie Kidd and Coia created most of its renowned work when, between 1945 and 1954, the practice was joined by Isi Metzstein and Andy MacMillan. Design control was passed from Coia to Metzstein and Macmillan in 1955 and the revived post-war practice continued Jack Coia's legacy of the patronage of the Roman Catholic church for who they designed a further 17 churches in Scotland. The rest of their work included mainly buildings in suburban settings in Glasgow and the Scottish New Towns as well as the now ill-fated St Peter's Seminary, Cardross (1958–66).

The church, St Paul's in the new town Glenrothes was one of Scotland's first New Towns and originally built to house miners from the newly established coal mine. After the mine closed, the town developed into an important industrial centre in Scotland's Silicon Glen, between 1961 and 2000. The church was built as a key cultural landmark in the town as well as to provide orientation in the landscape in what was a low density, sprawling town with little to hold it together. The building, although small, was intended to respond to issues of identity and orientation.

In a film featuring Andy MacMillan describing his and Metzstein's design approach he sets out their intentions, "We were interested in creating a memorable, simple, small building, white against the trees, maybe with a tower to suggest its 'churchiness'". After an extensive examination of the liturgical demands for the programme, they discovered that with the altar for the mass, the pulpit for preaching and the side altar for the devotions, that the sanctuary occupied a disproportionate area to the church and would compromise the congregational seating. To balance this they increased the seating by turning in the side walls to embrace the congregation. This gave the space a long processional axis. They then introduced the entrance and linked it to the presbytery, where the priest resides.

The approach to the church leads one along the external wall of the presbytery, an unwelcoming brick wall, while the domestic setting lessens the drama of the approach. Additionally the painted brick appears an odd choice in contrast to the bare faced brick expressed in their later work. After this journey one arrives at the confessional and past the baptism font. Moving through the choreographed spaces was intended to give the visitor time to adjust from the secular to the sacred interior.

The ritual of the mass was deemed to be the most important element, so the altar was placed within the tower which was top lit to provide natural light overhead. This theme of creating dynamic space with top lighting to illuminate the cross as the sun moves through its path, was a recurring technique in the practice's work. Additionally, the deep plan was one of the key architectural themes of Metzstein and MacMillan and this continued to inform their later works such as St Bride's, a monumental church with sculpted walls, inhabited with church effigies and light shafts.

→
The main church façade greets visitors with its asymmetrical cross, this became a landmark feature of MacMillan and Metztein's work.

Functional Buildings

Functional

The buildings' programme in this category is often driven by the processing of a raw material. Whether sand and cement to brick, raw nitro-cellulose to produce the dynamite cordite, or in the case of Caminto del Rey, a means of transporting the mining spoil out of the gorge. Under this typology architecture and technology are fused with their landscape. The two featured dams have significantly reshaped their surrounding topology and in the case of the Iznàjar Dam, the flooding of existing villages was carried out.

    The former chemical explosives factory covering 128 hectares of reclaimed estuarine saltmarsh in the north-west corner of the Hoo Peninsula, has been methodically mapped through an archaeological survey as part of the wider Historic Landscape Project. This is a crucial piece of documentation. Although the site has been left to rewild and is managed by tenant farmers, whose cattle and sheep prevent the grass turning to lignint, the site is vulnerable to development, being on the fringes of London. The scale of the site demonstrates the sense of how important it was to the character of the area and the local economy.

Headframe of the Sainte Marie Coalmine

Ronchamp, Franche-Comte, France

The Ronchamp Coal Mines covered a huge area located in the Vosges and Jura coal mining basins, in eastern France. They extended over three municipalities; Ronchamp, Champagney and Magny-Danigon. Operating for more than two centuries, from the mid-eighteenth century until the mid-twentieth century, they have profoundly changed the landscape, the economy and the local population.

The Sainte Marie Coalmine sits on the road leading up to Le Corbusier's Chapelle Notre Dame du Haut, just outside the small town of Ronchamp. The Roman Catholic chapel, Notre Dame du Haut, which was the last piece of architecture completed by the architect, Le Corbusier before his death in 1965 is said to be a master piece of sculptural qualities. The building makes up 17 of Le Corbusier's UNESCO listed sites. To reach the Chapel, which is the site of many architectural and spiritual pilgrimages one climbs a steeply ascending road passing the mine shaft, where the curved walls and up turned roof come into sight. Below the Chapel is the recently built Visitor Centre described as the 'rehabilitation of the site' designed by the Italian architect Renzo Piano and French landscape architect Michel Corajoud.

The Sainte Marie Coalmine was one of the major Ronchamp mines and was worked intermittently between 1866 and 1958, then finally closed. The concrete headframe was reinforced in 1924. On 29 March 2001, the headframe was listed as a French National Historical Monument.

The history of this particular mine commenced In 1830, when a survey was conducted atop Bourlémont Hill, near the eventual site of the Sainte Marie Coalmine. By the 1860s, the Stéphanien coal basin had been found and the Saint-Charles, Saint-Joseph, Sainte-Pauline and Sainte-Barbe mines were opened.

In 1863, it was decided that the Sainte Marie mine should be replaced by a new mineshaft to be dug to its west. The limits of the Ronchamp basin were not yet known and the new mine was located 1.4 kilometres to the west. Digging of the 3.5-metre-diameter mineshaft was begun in 1864 and proceeded with the help of six horses and a steam winch. Workers completed the digging in two years, having found the coalfield at a depth of 240 metres. The walls of the pit were constructed of Portland cement. Workers discovered another 60 metre layer of coal after further digging taking the shaft down to a depth of 359 metres.

Upon the nationalisation of French coal mines in 1946, under the provisional post-war government, initially led by Charles de Gaulle, Ronchamp Mining District was placed under the authority of Électricité de France (EDF), because it was too distant from the other large mining districts of France and it included a major thermal power plant.

After 1950, the Sainte Marie mine shaft, thought to still contain large masses of coal, was again discussed along with a neighboring site, the Tonnet mine shaft, whose coal reserves had already been judged to be exploitable. But the old constructions had to be cleaned up and drained of water, and new infrastructure had to be constructed. The cost of this project, undertaken by the mine's supporting committee was estimated at a billion francs.

The project stalled as EDF did not wish to invest further in the Ronchamp coal mines and was preparing to abandon the mining district. The Sainte Marie shaft closed permanently in 1958 and was filled in with schist, a coarse grained metamorphic rock which consists of layers of different minerals, with shale and topped with a concrete slab. It had been planned that the headframe should be demolished, but because of strong community attachment to it as part of their local heritage, it was saved in 1972 by a local resident, Dr. Marcel Maulini, who went on to establish a museum of mining in Ronchamp.

Curtis's & Harvey Ltd Explosives Factory

Cliffe, Medway, UK

Cliffe is a village which sits on the Hoo Peninsula, Kent reached from the Medway Towns by a four kilometre journey along the B2000. The village sits upon a low chalk escarpment overlooking the Thames Marshes and is an RSPB site.

As one leaves Cliffe the road turns into a rough track and here you can start one of the walks along a designated path way, the RSB1. From here or the sea wall path you see the first glimpses of the Curtis's & Harvey Explosive Factory which covers 128 hectares of the Cliffe Marshes. Stretching in front of you is a sight which is as surreal as the 20 degree centigrade February weather when I arrive at the site. A low run of a parade of pitched roofed structures compliment the horizon, which is punctuated with giraffe cranes, signaling Southend-on-Sea, on the other side of the Thames. The land is mainly made up of estuarine channels, with sheep and Icelandic horses grazing tufts, navigating the water courses and bunds and scars of bomb craters from World War Two.

The site, currently owned by the Port of London Authority and managed by tenant farmers, is out of bounds to the public due to its adjacency to the RSPB nature reserve and low lying marsh land which means that access is forbidden to protect nesting birds. In 2013 Historic England published an extensive survey of the factory remains, as well as an archaeological survey undertaken as part of the wider Hoo Peninsula Historic Landscape Project which is instrumental in influencing strategic decision making, in anticipation of future major development proposals. This site was mooted as a suitable plot for the Thames Estuary airport. Very little investigation has been made into the former explosive factory apart from its mention in Wayne Cocroft's publication, 'Dangerous Energy' (2000). The history of the site was laid down when Hay, Merrick & Co set up a small scale gunpowder storage facility in 1892. It was then acquired by Curtis's & Harvey Ltd who established a new chemical explosives

Functional Buildings

↗
The neatly sculpted step-sided earthwork traverses were built to enclose the more dangerous factory buildings up to the height of their eaves.

→
Interspersed between the factory features large water-filled borrow-pits created by extraction of earth for building protective traverses.

The reinforced concrete stalls comprising acetone recovery stoves (a solvent used to aid gelatinisation in some forms of cordite) were converted into pig stys as early as 1921.

factory. During the First World War it became a government controlled establishment manufacturing a range of propellant and blasting explosives with a primary focus on producing naval cordite (a compound used in ammunition). The enterprise was short lived, closing in 1920 due to the post-war reduction in the demand for munitions.

The layout of the First World War phase of the explosives factory survives largely as earthworks, concrete foundations and a few standing buildings. Most of the buildings from this phase have been demolished or reclaimed for reuse, leaving behind a complex of concrete floor slabs, protective earthwork traverse (blast protection mounds), embanked earthen trambeds and narrow drains. The geology underlying Cliffe Marshes consists of thick surface deposits of alluvium overlying Woolwich Beds of sands and clays and Thanet Beds of sand. These bedded sands seal layers of Upper Cretaceous chalk bedrock that underlie the entire peninsula.

When Curtis's & Harvey Ltd took over the site, it was a time of great change in the explosives industry with gunpowder rapidly giving way to chemical explosives, such as the new 'smokeless' cordite propellant, which gave better efficiency and accuracy. During the First World War a major government initiative expanded the site and it became known under its new name, 'HM Cordite Factory'.

The buildings were constructed along the eastern edge of the existing complex, to increase the capacity for production of cordite, this was followed by a rapid decline, with the end of the war triggering a cessation for official war work, a drop in demand of explosives and nationwide economic depression. In 1921 manufacturing at the site was terminated. By 1931 all of the former factories on Cliffe Marshes became under the ownership of the current owners, the Port London Authority and apart from the occasional limited military activity during World

↙
The older parts of the factory have grown organically whereas the First World War expansion of HM Cordite Factory site pay little attention to the pattern of drainage.

War Two the land has been untouched, save for use as grazing marshland. The layout, building styles and technology at Cliffe, would probably have been modeled on the existing cordite works at *Royal Gunpowder Factory* at Waltham Abbey, Essex. The advantages of the site at Cliffe provided easy access to London, room for expansion and a greenfield site, all ideal conditions for the chemical explosive works.

The extensive survey by Historic England drew attention to the remarkable extent and completeness of the plan of the factory, which represents the scale and nature of the manufacturing of explosives and the vast area demonstrating the economic impact the whole operation had on the local economy. The long building is the 1916 HM Cordite Factory, built of reinforced concrete which had a very limited application as a construction material in the British explosive industry, making Cliffe a rare survival of the material in this context. Most of the surviving examples are the roofless shells which were the former cordite drying stoves.

The survey was the first comprehensive piece of work to produce a detailed and accurate plan of the whole site. In many cases only the earthwork traverse, a blast protection mound surrounding an explosives building, survives to show the location of a building. In tracing the archeology of the site at times only a clear rectangular area of shorter discoloured grass betraying a concrete surface below the vegetation or the presence of a tank or group of manholes, would suggest the function of an area.

Some of the factory structures have been removed in more recent times as a result of the relocation and rebuilding of the sea wall in the 1980s. The marshland at Cliffe was reclaimed from original estuarine salt-marsh reclamations probably during the Roman times and by Dutch workmen and engineers in the seventeenth century, the drainage of the landscape seen today is generally attributed to medieval undertakings.

Dingleton Boiler

Melrose, Roxborough, UK

The disused Boilerhouse (1977) is located on the outskirts of Melrose. The striking north façade which is expressed through the inverted pyramidal sections, rises up from the sloping road, with the creep of conventional terraced housing developments encroaching on the building's periphery. When the Boilerhouse, designed by Peter Womersley, (1923-93) was completed in 1977, it won the Financial Times 'Commendation for Industrial Architecture,' applauded for its "refined and simple treatment". The elegant proportions of the building are expressed in its modular layout, with its four bay, rectangular plan with three graduating low pitched sections. The north elevation with its three recessed pyramidal forms is backed by ventilation louvres and divided by slender concrete fins.

The Boilerhouse was built as a separate building with an incinerator to serve the adjacent Dingleton Hospital, which was developed into flats in 2004. The hospital underwent many extensions and was the first British Psychiatric Hospital to adopt an 'open door' policy. This was supervised by Dr Maxwell Jones who commissioned Womersley to make improvements to the interior of the main hospital block. When the hospital was converted into 94 flats unfortunately Womersley's interiors were demolished. Aside from the Boilerhouse, Womersley enjoyed generous patronage from the NHS as a client, designing the Nuffield Transplant Unit at Edinburgh's Western General Hospital, a small admissions unit at the Herdmanflat clinic, near Edinburgh and a group practice surgery at Kelso.

Womersley spent most of his life working in the borders. After he completed his first commission for his brother, *Farnley Hey* in Yorkshire, he relocated to a peaceful rural spot in Gattonside near Melrose where he designed his own home and office.

The Edinburgh practice, 'Studio Dub' have acquired the Boilerhouse with plans to convert it into four dwellings, using the precedent of the Spanish architect, Ricardo Bofill's *La Fabrica*.

→
The building was described by Historic Scotland as a 'monolithic landmark of functionality'. The property has planning permission to create five properties carved out of the sculptural concrete and reuse the existing chimney for wood-burning stoves.

Backwater Reservoir
Angus, Scotland, UK

The Backwater Reservoir can be reached by taking the B951 turn-off from the A93, around eight kilometres south of Spittal of Glenshee or from the A926 at Kirriemuir to the south-east. The reservoir, opened in 1969 was designed by the Edinburgh based architects Baxter Clark and Paul, with the engineers Babtie, Shaw and Morton.

The vast stretch of water three kilometres long with a peak capacity of 24 million cubic metres is held back with an embankment which measures 42 metres high and 570 metres long. The landscape behind the embankment resembles a well-manicured contemporary park. Built into the sharply sloping bank are the maintenance houses all carefully constructed out of local quarried stone, with their roofs flush to the terrace levels as they drop down to the pump station. The considered architectural details are articulated at every junction, roof detail and wall. What is surprising is that the dam is a wholly public space. The banks can be picnicked upon and enjoyed as if open countryside. The shaped slopes and structures which interlock with the landscape are similar to the Highland bothys which sit sensitively within the landscape. The overspill channel is a huge stepped cascade resembling a twentieth century version of an Italian renaissance garden.

The reservoir's only purpose is to provide drinking water supplying Angus, Dundee and parts of Perth and Kinross. Backwater, together with the smaller Lintrathen Reservoir four kilometres to the south, is capable of supplying some 300,000 people with drinking water. An unclassified road runs across the spillway and embankment before following the east bank of the water, which continues a further two kilometres before petering out. As you enter the road the valve house rises up from the water, an elegant concrete structure with a butterfly roof and pronounced concrete gutters. The placing of renewable energy infrastructure projects within areas of various protective listings is controversial. Recent applications for the reservoir have included large scale wind energy developments. In assessing the landscape the architect Sylvia Crowe wrote in her early seminal book, *Landscapes of Power* (1958) that "constructions conceived as self-contained problems of design have been the bane of the landscape for the past century, but there is at last a dawning realization that every building, from a single house to a new town, from a small factory to a nuclear power station, must be considered in relation to its site and as part of the complex pattern of our national landscape."

In assessing the impact of a proposed building on the landscape a similar process to the proposal for a high rise building within an urban context is at play. The Landscape and Visual Impact Assessment (LVIA) process provides a formal method for assessing landscape context. However, the formality of the LVIA process limits interpretation of landscape to those things which can be easily measured or quantified and deals primarily with visual aspects, leaving out the more enigmatic qualities to do with emotions, history, culture, narrative and memories.

In assessing recent applications for the Backwater site attention has been drawn to the identity of the area which is described as forming a transition between the lowlands and highlands around the Highland Boundary Fault. The northern part of the site displays characteristics of wild land which national planning policy and guidance seeks to safeguard. The Backwater Glendamff corridor is an important part of the setting of the Cairngorms National Park as it both frames and focuses views towards the Munro summits of Mayar and Driesh.

→ The butterfly valve station stands in the middle of the Backwater Reservoir at the foot of the Glenshee Mountains.

→
The dam stretches north into Glen Damff, the two-and-a half mile long ribbon of water flanked with side by hills, moorland and forestry maintained by Scottish water. The overflow channel or spillway sits downstream.

Functional Buildings

Water Tower

Ezhupunna, Kerala, India

The Water Tower is sited between Kochi and the backwaters of the south Indian state, Kerala, which is threaded with 44 rivers feeding its lush green landscape and is flanked on the west by the Arabian Sea and on the east by the Western Ghats.

Next to the Water Tower sits a Hindu funeral pyre. Perhaps the adjacency of the essential elements of life, fire and water, are no accident. Both the storage tank and funeral pyre sit on the periphery of the small town. The Tower's monumental skeletal modular frame is similar to a Sol LeWitt sculpture with the repeated grid of eight by seven bays.

The Tower is administered by the Kerala Water Authority (KWA). The state owned organisation provides a piped water supply to the state, but the supply is characterised by poor planning in terms of sustainability, technology choice and design optimisation resulting in source and system failures. The operation and maintenance of the schemes are very poor and there is little chance for improvement due to lack of will and poor cost of recovery.

Despite high rainfall and numerous water sources, Kerala suffers from the lowest per capita share of water. In addition most of the water from the rivers is unfit for drinking, due to high levels of bacteriological pollution, as well as pollution due to industrial, domestic wastes, pesticides and fertilisers. The state is bestowed with enviable natural resources, a rainfall that averages as high as 3,000 mm a year. As one of the most densely populated states in the country, it has high indicators of health and social development and its model for development has been hailed as an important indicator for other states to follow. However, recent evidence shows that high population density, industrialisation, urbanisation, mismanagement of water resources and vagaries of climate change have taken their toll on the water resources.

Currently the state's water supply is entirely dependent on rainfall, which shows seasonal and regional variations that lead to occasional floods and droughts. Rainfall is also the main source of groundwater recharge and influences the water levels in the subsurface and deeper aquifers. There is a large variation in rainfall between districts and recent evidence shows that there has been a decline, especially in the north, over the years along with changes in the form and timing of the rains. Experts attribute this change in rainfall patterns to climate change and changes in land use patterns and forest cover.

As high as 62 percent of the households in Kerala depend on well water to meet their water needs and the state has a very high density of open wells with 250 open wells per km². In rural Kerala, only 29.5 percent of households get drinking water from an improved source while the proportion is as high as 80 percent or more for most of the other bigger states.

→
Mixing art and functionality, engineers started designing water towers that would either blend in with the landscape or ornate designs were also fashionable.

Functional Buildings

Stewartby Brickworks

Stewartby, Bedfordshire, UK

The Estonian born architect Louis Khan, was one of the great masters of modern architecture, his most revered works being sculpted with brick and concrete. It was his belief that the humble brick could be part of a greater architecture, expressed in his often quoted idiosyncratic statement, "Even a brick wants to be something. It aspires. Even a common, ordinary brick, wants to be something more than it is." His belief in the power of the material to speak for itself in architecture, created some great monolithic masonry structures such as the *Institute of Management* in Ahmedabad, India, (1974).

    The impressive scale of the Stewartby Brickworks, is testimony to its importance played in supplying the UK building industry. By 1936, Stewartby had become the largest brickworks in the world, employing 2,000 people and producing 500 million bricks per annum. The development of the brickworks has been a major factor in forging the character of the local communities of Bedfordshire. In 1926 Stewartby produced 118 million bricks and work had started on the model 'garden village' to house employees. Based on the strong moral and religious beliefs of the Stewartby family, the village of Wootton Pillinge was transformed into Stewartby Model village. As well as providing low-cost housing, the employees benefited from better pay and working conditions and the company benefited in turn from having a greater degree of control over its workforce. The village became known as Stewartby in 1937 and was later given parish status. After World War Two, when labour was in short supply, many workers were encouraged to emigrate from other countries

←
At the time of taking the photograph only four of the original 32 chimneys remain on site, standing up to 70 meters in height. All of the chimneys will be demolished despite Historic England vetoing the decision.

↗
Some of the bricks on the vaults have been pushed out to stand proud of the façade probably due to the intense heat from the furnace, causing the heave.

→
The steel ribbon straps around the chimney are designed to prevent bowing of the structure. The chimney has been constructed using courses of header and stretcher bricks.

Functional Buildings

← ↗
The pile of coal slag and ash dust were probably cleared out from the blast furnaces. The brick layout on the floor shows the range of London bricks, some of them London vernacular. These would be the seconds which did not fire evenly thus the dappled colouring.

to work in the industry, initially from Commonwealth countries and Poland, and then from Italy and parts of Asia.

Stewartby was still said to be the largest brickworks in the world in 1979. There were then two other working brickworks in Bedfordshire at Ridgmont and Kempston Hardwick. These have since ceased production, so that Stewartby was the sole working Bedfordshire brickworks, until 2008.

The sculptural elegance of the building's forms is striking, the long tunnels which house the kilns have brick lined arched chambers with side vents through which the heat is drawn along the kiln. The Hoffman Kilns are square ended and comprise two parallel rows of chambers. They are said to be of the type specifically designed for the Fletton industry, producing the stalwart brick or industry workhorse as it is often described. Fletton is the generic name given to bricks made from lower Oxford clay which have a low fuel cost due to the carbonaceous content of the clay.

Beneath the floors are interconnecting flues through which air is drawn by the chimney. Four of the 32 original chimneys remain on the site, standing up to 70m tall. The four chimneys taper and are banded with iron straps for added stability. In recent years steel platforms with access steps have been attached along with monitoring equipment for smoke quality. In the end the fact that the brickworks could not meet modern standards of waste emissions forced the site to close.

The structures are a symbol of the brickwork industry in Bedfordshire dating back to the 1930s. Current plans to turn the site into a mixed-use development with 4,000 homes, have been approved including permission to demolish all of the chimneys and rebuild one with the letters, Stewartby down the side. A recommendation by Historic England, that the Brickworks should be listed in view of their iconic role in bringing industrialisation to a rural landscape was not approved.

Caminito del Rey

Desfiladero de los Gaitanes, El Chorro, Spain

The spectacular nature of the engineering feat of El Caminito del Rey is matched by its surrounding landscape and dramatic scenery. The walkway is built through the gorge called 'Desfiladero de los Gaitanes'. It lies in the Province of Malaga, surrounded by the mountain range, Serranía de Ronda. It separates the plains Camplillos, Teba and Antequera in the northern part of the province from the Guadalhorce valley and the fields of Cámara in the south. The path stretches between two gorges of limestone and dolomite, canyons, a large valley, and along pathways or boardwalks. It was built to provide workers at the hydroelectric power plants at Chorro Falls and Gaitanejo Falls with a means to cross between them, to provide for the transport of materials and to help facilitate inspection and maintenance of the channel. The construction began in 1901 and was finished in 1905. King Alfonso XIII crossed the walkway in 1921 for the inauguration of the Conde del Guadalhorce dam and it became known by its present name, El Caminito del Rey, which in English translates as The Kings's Little Pathway.

Much fanfare surrounded the reopening of the Caminito del Rey after a major restoration project funded by the EU. The original path was constructed of concrete slabs and rested on steel sections supported by stanchions cantilevered from the rock face. The rusted steel and general deterioration of the structure over the years, meant that there were numerous sections where part or all of the concrete slabs had collapsed. The result was large open-air gaps bridged only by narrow steel beams or other supports. Few of the original handrails existed, although a safety wire ran the length of the path.

Before the restoration project, the rock face and remnants of the path had become a popular climbing area for daring hikers who would risk their lives free climbing over what remained of the walkways. Several people lost their lives on the walkway and after two fatal accidents in 1999 and 2000, the local government closed both entrances. The restored paths are one metre in width and rise over 100 metres above the river below. Passage through the current walkways between the valleys, which has to be booked well in advance due to its popularity, has been given an up-grade complete with glass viewing platforms and contemporary suspension bridges traversing the gorge, which hover directly over the original paths.

The El Chorro railway station which serves the small village and is the nearest public transport to arrive at the walkway has a cluster of hotels and bars and was built to link this relatively underdeveloped area which relied on farming and livestock with the major coastal towns such as Malaga and Marbella. In order to supply energy demands coming from the coast in the 1950s and 1960s the hydroelectric dam which can be seen from the gorge, was created to meet the growing demand.

→
The architect of the project Luis Machuca, who is Head of the Architecture and Town Planning Department at the local County Council was awarded a National Award for the project team's consideration of the cultural heritage and the landscape.

Iznájar Dam

Andalucia, Spain

The Iznájar Reservoir, known locally as the 'Embalse de Iznájar' is the largest reservoir in the Andalucían Region. It was opened by General Franco on the third of June 1969 and occupies land in the provinces of Córdoba, Granada and Málaga. The style of architecture resembles the formal language of 1930s architecture, with Italian futurist tendencies, relating to shared fascist values. Inside one of the dam access shafts is a mosaic of a picturesque scene of the surrounding area.

When the dam was constructed, over a ten-year period in the 1960s, it was the largest dam in Spain requiring 1.4 million cubic metres of concrete. At the foot of the dam rose the most important hydroelectric power station in Andalucía, producing one hundred million kilowatt hours per year with intercommunications throughout the south of the peninsula. The construction of the dam meant the expropriation of the best cultivable land in the municipality, which caused the displacement of innumerable Iznájos (the name for residents of the Iznájar region).

The construction of the reservoir modified the surrounding land, its main nucleus now stands as a small peninsula that is connected to the land to the north and south by two long bridges. The dam not only brought about a change in the physical environment, but a shift in economic activities, population settlements and infrastructure, extending the original town Iznájar, creating a satellite town with an inland beach and waterfront. When the lake is low, usually during the summer months, you can see parts of the old town such as the old bridge and ruins.

The crest length of the dam is 406 metres and an elevation of 426 metres.

↖ ↗
The construction work for the Iznájar dam, on the course of the Genil river was finished in 1969. It has a height of 101 m over the river bed. The Pump Station has a large cast iron crest on the front façade.

The lake covers 3,000 hectares though 200 hectares of irrigated land and 150,000 olive trees were flooded, the water has provided for an additional 65,000 hectares of irrigation. Its capacity exceeds 950 million cubic metres of water destined for domestic consumption and has more than 100 kilometres of shore and is over 30 kilometres in length.

The vision of this technological advancement was described as a political technology, which fed into the vision of Francoist Spain. The assemblage of technological advancement, the reshaping of the landscape, in parts the submerging of existing villages, was made in the advancement of the nation's identity under the reign of the dictator, Franco (1939–1975).

Documents on the building of the dams contained no records of contestation of the expropriation of the flooded land largely because the dictatorship's information apparatus censored any kind of opposition to mainstream views. The transition from a uniform electricity network in Spain meant a conjoining of nineteenth century ideals of supporting farmers through irrigation and the change of scale in energy production that took place after the Spanish Civil War (1936–1939). The construction of dams played a political role in restructuring the lives of the peasant farmer where small plot farming was replaced through the agricultural policy of an interventionist government, with a view to boosting the economy of Spain. Water works were seen as symbolising state power. There was an assumption that certain regions would be sacrificed in the interest of the national economy. Such assumptions began to crumble in the 1970s, hence the questioning of the hydraulic paradigm.

By the 1980s when the vision of hydropower projects began to be questioned, its share of the electricity production of Spain, had fallen from 78% of the market in 1940 to 43% in 1980. The discourses which made hydropower compelling during the dictatorship lost their power during the transition to democracy.

Bernat Klein Studio

Selkirk, Scottish Borders, UK

When I visited *High Sunderland*, Bernat Klein's daughter was packing up the last remaining objects, some of which included her father's paintings after the recent sale of the house. *High Sunderland*, (1957) had been the family home of the Serbian textile designer Bernat Klein designed by the architect Peter Womersley (1923–93). The single storey modernist timber frame house designed on a modular plan of 14 by five bays, is reminiscent of the Californian Case Study houses with its flat roof and composition of glazing and brightly coloured panels. The house sits in sparsely populated landscape overlooking fields of grazing cheviot sheep. It was here that Klein, the textile designer set up his home and studio in Scotland and was taken up by some of Europe's leading fashion houses, such as House of Dior and Chanel.

Klein operated first as a designer in the Border's weaving factories and then set up his own studio, *Bernat Klein Ltd*. The use of exuberant colour as a key component of his designs, was described in his book *Eye for Colour*, (1965) inspired by artists such as Georges Seurat, Paul Klee and Oscar Kokoschka. Klein's textiles featured strongly in *High Sunderland*, which he commissioned after Klein had visited *Farnley Hey*, twenty years earlier, a private house near Huddersfield, designed for Wormesley's brother.

After completing the house, Klein then commissioned Womersley to build his studio in 1971 which was a short walk from *High Sunderland*. I took that walk which Klein would have made so often through mulched leaf covered ground, past a wooden hut, built into the wooded slope. Klein had a deep interest in design, art and painting born, not just through his textiles, but also his love for architecture and he became Womersley's most important client.

The Studio is an expressive piece of architecture. Womersley's work has been discussed as additive and subtractive. Here it seems to lie in between. The building was carefully sited so that the removal of only one beech tree was necessary. To enhance the building's setting the site was extensively contoured and the building set upon a brick plinth.

The building is rectangular in plan and spread over two floors. One enters from a bridge accessed from the hillside which brings you into the first floor. The staircase is expressed as a central core of engineering bricks, which extrudes through the roof serving a roof terrace. Ribbon windows wrap around the perimeter, allowing light to flood in, creating the experience of being embedded in the surrounding woods. The building is a varied palette of brick, timber cladding and concrete.

The lower ground level sits on a generous brick plinth with recessed windows providing a deep ledge offering space for sitting. It is a striking building in a rural setting, with its expressed horizontal lines further emphasised by introducing an elongated floating external concrete frame. The upper floor was originally carpeted in white and furnished so that it could be used as four independent zones: central for servicing and exhibitions; northern for painting; western for meetings and south-eastern for informal discussions around a fireplace. All the corner windows are frameless and mitred so as to enhance the views and to accentuate the suspended floating character of the upper studio.

In 1973 the Studio received both an RIBA Award and the Edinburgh Architectural Association Centenary Medal. Klein sold the studio separately in 2002 and sadly by 2013 it was listed as a building 'at risk' by Historic Scotland, due to the current owner's lack of maintenance leaving the structure in a state of neglect.

Architecture of Leisure

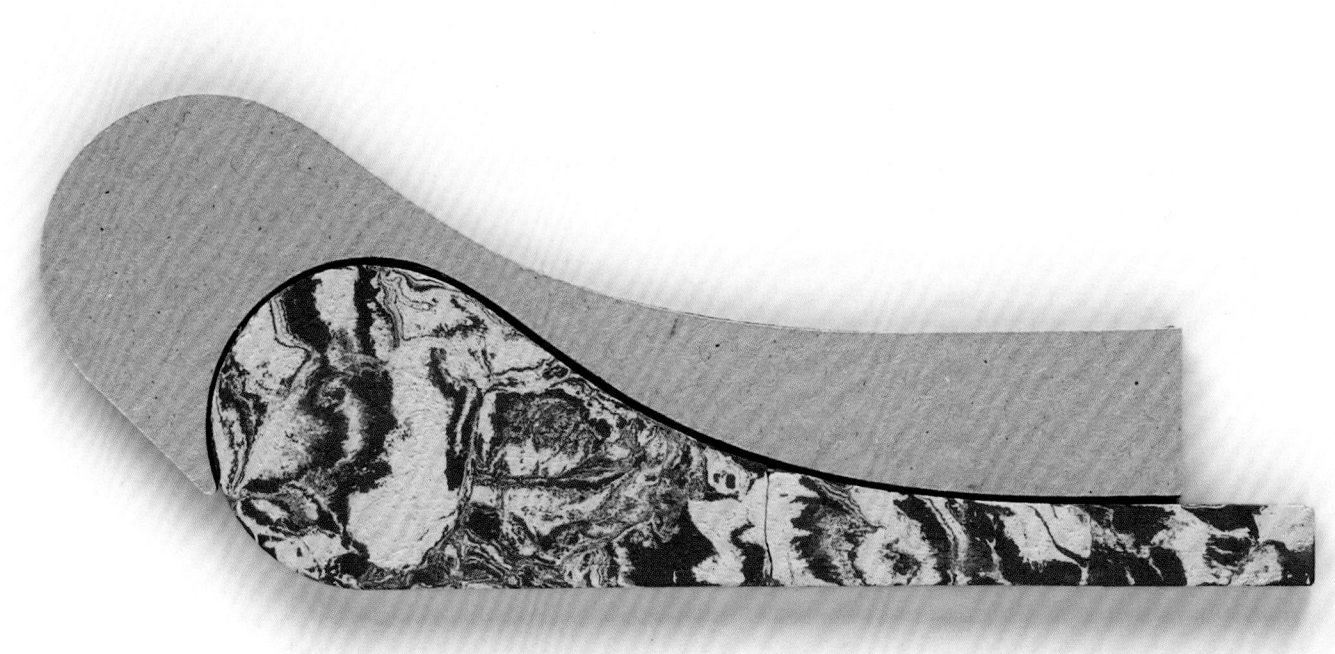

Leisure

Leisure, as an architectural type came into its own with the introduction of industrialisation, expendable income and with it, free time. The Cliftonville Bathhouse maps those changes from the rise of the affluent class to the demise of seaside tourism as a result of the overseas package holiday.

The proximity to water in the case of the Passenger Terminal, Bentota Beach Hotel or Lido sees a variety of design approaches where architecture meets the littoral condition of water and land. Cliftonville was spread over four levels, the lower excavated from the chalk cliffs and in 1928 the Lido was added which could accommodate 1000 bathers and be filled and emptied everyday with the ebb and flow of the tide. The Baths is reputed to be the only known example of a sea bathing establishment which was dug out of the cliffs and as a result altered the local topography. Even though the Passenger Terminal looks as robust as it did since its inception, further down the coast there is the memory of the failed testing of the *Turner Contemporary* competition wining scheme by Snøhetta & Spence. When struck by a freak wave, the trial construction for the gallery built on the pier floated out to sea, thus putting paid to any sea facing edifice.

Bentota Beach Hotel

Bentota, Sri Lanka

After visiting Geoffrey Bawa's home in Lunanganga, and his brother, Bevis Bawa's house with its extensively laid out gardens called the *Brief* a few kilometres apart, hidden behind a wall of construction hoarding I discovered The Bentota Beach Hotel (1967–69) when returning to the coast. The hotel commands a significant position, sitting on a spit of land which divides the long sandy beach of the Indian Ocean fringed with palm trees, with the Bentota River which winds its way along mangrove-clad banks toward the sea. The architectural historian David Robson describes the hotel as, "arguably one of Bawa's most important buildings, which resolved some of the key dilemmas facing a designer of resort hotels". Bawa successfully reconciles the design of the modern hotel with the culture and tradition of its wider context. Robson describes the building's influences as bringing together the diverse references such as the medieval manor house, the lost world of ancient palaces and colonial villas. Bawa, who initially trained as a lawyer, returned to his native Sri Lanka after studying at the Architectural Association, London. His method of working was to collaborate with a developer thus investing and taking a share of the profits from the joint enterprises.

On meeting the architect Channa Daswatte, who worked closely with Bawa, he describes the project to restore the hotel, "The Bentota Beach will be a project similar to the Ena house except on site", (the Bawa foundation moved, stone by stone, the Ena de Silva House from Colombo, at risk of demolition, to its new site on the Bawa estate at Lunaganga). Daswatte

 The Sri Lankan artist Laki Senanayake was given numerous commissions by Bawa which included batiks, paintings and sculptures. He was also a skilled landscape architect and provided all the trees for the jungle hotel Kandalama for which he also created the regal metal owl soaring over the hotel premises.

 Bawa treated each staircase in his architecture as a sculptural object. His references were broad, linking both western historical ideas with traditional Sri Lankan temple architecture.

↗
Bawa was credited with the design of the first infinity pools. Here the pool incorporates crevices of natural rocks.

Architecture of Leisure

continues, "Everything that can be reused will be reused to make it as authentic as possible to the original building. All the timber work, stone, etc, will be renovated. However, some elements of the building which were destroyed during an unfortunate refurbishment in the 1990's will be re-established, except for the shutters, which of course will firmly remain surrounding my house!" Daswatte is also overseeing the collection of the Bawa archive of which parts have been recently acquired by the *M+ Gallery* in the Kowloon Cultural District, Hong Kong.

Bawa's skill lay in creating a powerful sense of theatricality expressed within the architectural promenade through his buildings. This he achieves with the skill of a choreographer. Guests arriving from Colombo, first glimpse the hotel's roof tops above a canopy of coconut trees, then after having crossed the Bentota River arrive at the massive stone bastion, which looks like it's been roughly hewn from rock, are swept under a 'porte-cochère' from here a stone staircase takes guests up to the reception area with a batik lined ceiling. From here the central courtyard with ornamental pool stretches out surrounded by a trio of temple trees with views across the Indian Ocean.

Bawa combined the materials rough granite, polished concrete, terracotta, dark stained timber, warm handloom ceilings, samara ochre coloured soffits, providing the interiors with a sense of warmth and continuity with the past. Bentota was built during a period of restricted imports of building materials, therefore local craftsmen built all the furniture which was designed in Bawa's studio and fabrics were woven by Barbara Sansoni's convent girls. Sansoni, a distant cousin of Bawa, was a self-trained artist. During the 1960s she established weaving factories with the nuns of the 'Good Shepherd Convent' near Bentota, which provided a source of fabrics for Bawa's projects.

Unfortunately after 30 years of survival in its original form, in the 1980s the government withdrew its shares in the hotel and it was subsequently purchased by Keells Hotel Management. The hotel chain undertook a dramatic project of modernisation making a host of insensitive moves, such as replacing the terracotta roof tiles with green metal sheeting. The hotel was closed in 2016 and at the time of visiting was undergoing restoration. A team of security guards vigilantly manned the entrance, but with gentle persuasion I was allowed to proceed as far as the courtyard, where the stone floor tiles were each individually numbered. Retreating to the ocean side there was no barrier of guards so access was completely unrestricted, and I was free to roam the building, noticing a recent flyer for the auction of all the contents including the original Bawa furniture. The hotel has now reopened with attempts to revisit the original artistic touches commissioned by Bawa, but if the new batik ceiling finished in garish pinks and reds is anything to go by, Bawa purists might be disappointed.

←
The Colonial Dutch style hotel is set in 30 acres of groves of coconut palm trees.

Gala Fairydean Stadium

Netherdale, Galashiels, UK

In 1944 the architects Alan Reiach and Robert Hurd published *Building Scotland, Past and Future* which was a forward looking celebration of the status of architecture in Scotland as well as a bid to promote a brave approach to Scotland's planning post-war. But currently fewer than 200 buildings erected after World War Two have been listed for their special architectural or historic interest. As a prologue to the 1950s, Reiach and Hurd called on architects to look to the potential of modern architecture to improve lives and enlighten our built environment. They cautioned however against losing a sense of what they termed the local character.

One of their featured architects was Peter Womersley, (1923–1993). Amongst his many commissions in the Borders of Scotland is the Football stadium (1963–4), given the otherworldly name, Fairydean. Its name is based on the local connection found in Sir Walter Scott's novel *The Monastery: a Romance*, (1820) set in the Glen of Allen on the River Tweed near Galashiels, which is known as the 'Fairy Dean'. Womersley worked with the engineers Ove Arup to form the highly distinctive construction comprising four V-sectioned vertical fins supporting the wedge-shaped stand and cantilevered canopy. At either end of the stadium are turnstiles with inverted pyramidal canopies. Open-tread concrete stairs, give access to the upper levels with raked concrete and timber-board seating. The changing rooms and bar are on the ground level. The substantial concrete canopy hovering over the seating is cantilevered so that when viewed from the pitch, it appears to defy gravity and balance precariously on the thin back edge of the seating terrace. The building was described by *Architecture Today*, in 1965 as a "geometrical composition of unusual interest and subtlety".

Peter Womersley was the subject of a biographical survey in 2006 with a number of his private and public buildings newly listed, including Gala Fairydean, Galashiels and his own house at Gattonside, called *The Rig* (1956–7). Womersley ran a small practice from the Borders, but would nonetheless make a name for himself with highly individualistic, almost lyrical, designs for a range of building types which explore the sculptural properties of raw concrete. Gala Fairydean Football Club was formed in 1908. The club's first stand was demolished in 1963 and Womersley's futuristic but still relatively modest 750-seat stand was opened in November 1964 at a time of increasing success for Gala Fairydean. The building has been altered slightly since then including the addition of brick between the concrete columns to form an extension to the bar. The building's listing category was changed from B to A and list description updated as part of the sporting buildings thematic study by Historic Scotland (2012–13).

→
The side elevation demonstrates the powerful angular forms and the focus on the cantilever and buttresses in tension.

Las Cabañas
Rute, Cordoba, Spain

← The cabins are constructed to a high standard using kiln dried pine planks which have weathered to a dark brown and grey. The simple corrugated roof overhang provides protection from rainfall and sun.

The mise-en-scene of the cabin standing within a remote wood has become a metaphor for an idyllic pastoral life, the nineteenth century Naturalist, Philosopher and Social reformer Henry Thoreau, in his attempt to create a greater understanding of our life on earth through an engagement with the natural world, spent two years, two days and two hours living in a log cabin he built on the shore of Walden Pond, Massachusetts. His account of the experience was told in, *Life in the Woods* (1854). But the disruptor to this idyll is the basis for many a fairytale, acted out in *Hansel and Gretel* who were lured by the promise of nourishment into the wooden cabin of the thinly disguised witch, or its use as a horror film genre, where for example the film of the same title 'Cabin in the Woods' (2012) pulled out all the classic tropes from the introduction of the cellar, with it inferences of the subterranean, to associations of isolation and a lack of communication with the outside world.

Another more sanguine example I am reminded of is the *Cabanon* (1951) designed by Le Corbusier, which he built just outside Roqubrune Cap-Martin, overlooking the Mediterranean, as a birthday present for his wife Yvonne Gallis. But also as an antagonistic act to rival the Irish architect Eileen Gray who had already established herself on the site and built the much lauded Villa E-1027. The land was gifted to the architect by the local land owner, Mr Rebutato who ran a bistro called Etoile de Mer and in exchange Le Corbusier designed a series of holiday cabins.

Las Cabañas remain a mystery as to who commissioned them. They stand next to Iznajàr lake and were probably part of Franco's dam building programme where workers were provided with good quality accommodation, a church and recreational activities situated nearby to the site of the dam or a holiday camp to take advantage of the lake activities.

The camp sits amongst the pine trees, clad with split logs around a wooden structural frame. Each cabin has apertures articulated with pronounced frames with openings for both the upper and lower bunks. The carefully planned siting of Las Cabañas, amongst the pines sit on leveled plots which terraces the landscape, with shared B-B-Q pits. They are constructed on a concrete slab base with a toilet and shower, and bunks in each cabin. It is clear from the dimensions of the bunk beds that they were designed to accommodate children.

The lake is the largest in Andalucía and the dam, when constructed over fifty years ago in the 1960s was the largest in Spain requiring 1.4 million cubic metres of concrete. The reservoir was opened by General Franco on 3 June 1969. As the now A-333 bridges were not completed in time, a ferry service was laid on. The lake covers 3,000 hectares. Although 200 hectares of irrigated land and 150,000 olive trees were flooded, the water has provided for an additional 65,000 hectares of irrigation downstream. Swimming and non-motorised watersports are permitted on the lake.

→
Each cabin sits on a concrete base with a tiled external terrace area. The blanket of pine needles allows only certain grasses to take seed such as the Spanish Stipa gigantea, which thrives in sharply drained, stony soil of scrub covered hillsides.

Olau Passenger Ferry

Sheerness, Isle of Sheppey, UK

Although Sheerness is only 80 kilometres from London, it appears to have a unique identity far removed from the capital, very much tied up with its recent history. Its naval dockyard was officially closed in 1970 with the loss of a large number of jobs and with it a sense of continuity with the town's history. Separated from the mainland by The Swale, where the low lying southern marshlands of Sheppey, the Isle of Harty and Isle of Elmley, sit virtually at sea level. These areas are combed with rivulets and estuarine channels making them ideal bird habitats, but vulnerable to flooding.

    On the north west tip of Sheppey, lies Sheerness. Currently the main source of employment in Sheerness is the import-export commercial dock, Peel Ports, which took over the port from HM Navy. On its north side just below the nineteenth century Garrison Fort sits the Olau Passenger Ferry where the Thames and Medway meet. The architecture of the terminal is a veritable Archigram structure. Its kit like covered walkway clad with corrugated sheeting sits on a concrete footing, with inverted trusses, the structure is barely weathered. The ferry opened in 1974 when the Danish company Olau Line started a car/passenger ferry service from Sheerness to Vlissingen in the Netherlands and from Copenhagen to Aalborg, Denmark. In 1977 Olau attempted to start a service from Sheerness to Dunkerque, but lack of demand meant that by the end of the 1970s the company was heavily in debt and in 1979 Ole Lauritzen was forced to sell 50% of the Olau Line to the West Germany based TT-Line.

    Sheerness has suffered most recently from lack of investment. In the latter part of the nineteenth century the town expanded significantly, due to the importance of the naval dockyard as a result of the Crimean War and was viewed as the best equipped naval dockyard on the English east coast. Within the yard is the renowned building, the Boat Store, built between

← The standardised forms of the jetty complete with port hole gasket windows, playfully alternate the horizontal and vertical ribs on the corrugated sheets which are riveted together.

← The passenger holding space is connected with moveable pneumatic drivers to allow the area to adapt to tides and different water levels.

1856 and 1869. It is one on the earliest examples of an iron portal frame which makes it of extremely high significance as a Grade 1 listed building and an example of pioneering structural techniques employed by the Royal Engineers. These structural innovations were adopted in the late nineteenth century architecture especially in Chicago where the first skyscrapers were constructed.

The terminal at the Port of Sheerness plays a significant part in the Isle of Sheppey's economy. Covering more than 1.5 million square metres, it is one of the largest foreign car importers in the UK, as well as handling thousands of tonnes of fruits from all over the world. Stacks of Chiquita banana containers line the port front. Inexpensive land and good infrastructure, including a rail network that branches off the main passenger line, have attracted industries to the port area, including producers of pharmaceuticals, steel, sausages and even garden gnomes. The ports of Sheerness and Chatham form the core terminals of Peel Ports' London Medway cluster. They act as the statutory harbour authority along a 30 kilometre stretch of the Rivers Medway and Swale. The sites handle a vast array of cargo and can process *RoRo* 'roll on, roll off' and *LoLo* cargo, vessels, which use a crane to load and unload cargo.

The Medway has the largest catchment of any river in southern England. Its reach and strategic location give it a wide-ranging influence. Positioned on the Thames Estuary and within easy reach of Northern Europe, it also has deep-water access, which is perfect for international ships of varying sizes. The abandoned Passenger Ferry Terminal stands as a symbol of the varying fortunes of a major port and the changes in patterns of trade, tourism and of naval warfare, power and strategy.

Cliftonville Lido

Margate, Kent, UK

The Kent seaside town of Margate has experienced a recent up lift in its fortunes with the introduction of the highspeed railway, the Javelin, from London Kings Cross and the arrival of the *Turner Contemporary* art gallery designed by David Chipperfield Architects. Its form, a cluster of shed like volumes, looks out to the North Sea. If you continue along the coast towards Cliftonville you will find the tired and sea battered remnants of the Cliftonville Lido. The Lido was added to the elaborate system of underground baths and heated bathing pools called the Clifton Baths.

These are unique as they are the only known example of a sea bathing establishment to be dug out of the cliffs, altering the existing topography. The earliest reference to therapeutic seawater bathing in Margate was in 1736. This was followed by the invention of the bathing machine modesty hood in Margate in the 1750s and later by the *Royal Sea Bathing Hospital* on the west side of town in 1793. The Lido was the last addition to the bath houses, which sits within the Cliftonville Clifftop conservation area and was granted a Grade 2 listing in 2008.

Very little of the intricate subterranean arrangement of bath houses providing both hot and cold baths, bathing machines, libraries and refreshments, still exist. A recent Thanet Planning research document described the buildings as "offering exclusivity, privacy and an atmosphere of the Gothick Sublime, somewhat in the spirit of Mary Shelley's Frankenstein of 1818." The baths, completed in 1826 were built by a Margate solicitor, John Boys (1782–1849), who was instrumental in other Margate projects such as the Stone Pier and Hawley Square.

The ambition of Boys resulted in his commissioning of two breakwaters out from the cliff base to form an artificial bay, levelling the chalk reefs which sat off from the cliff face, causing sand to build up in the bay. He also remodeled the coast line by cutting a series of terraces into the cliff which he covered in rustic masonry to resemble fortifications. Below these structures, were a series of brick and flint lined tunnels. A series of varied bathing offers led the user through the barrel vaulted tunnels which covered a cold plunge pool where ladies and children could bathe naked. A dam at the end of the pool retained seawater at low tide, whilst the pool was also fed by a fresh water stream. The dome housed the storage area for the bathing machines with eight arches leading to tunnels around the perimeter, similar to a railway roundhouse. Some of these tunnels are now full of rubble.

The baths offered an exclusive up-market establishment and the area was named Cliftonville after the baths. In the nineteenth century Margate attracted a wider socio-economic resident and the baths became less exclusive switching to cater for a broader demographic. A laundry and indoor swimming pool were added in the 1880s and later a cinema. In 1919 the promotor of the fairground *Dreamland*, bought the site. He remodeled the building on the 'lido' style of the twentieth century with open air pools and a subterranean theatre. The outdoor lido was built over the breakwater with a tiered promenade. Beneath were changing rooms for 200 swimmers. The 1920s structure is constructed of steel frames and the original flint and brick building from Boy's time and the nineteenth century alterations can be seen behind and beneath the later additions.

A major storm in 1978 damaged the Lido and Margate's traditional pier, which was subsequently demolished. This year is often cited as marking the downturn in the local tourism economy. The tidal pool has been infilled, although the nineteenth century structures remain in good condition. This is one of the earliest surviving seawater bathing establishments in the country.

The Colonia Principi di Piemonte
Lido, Venice, Italy

← ↗
The principle building of the camp houses the ramp which runs the full height of the building. The chapel with the remnants of a ceramic tiled iron cross on the travertine altar was probably added when the building was renovated in 1961.

The Colonia Principi di Piemonte lies on Venice's Lido in Alberoni, built between 1936–37. Original photographs of the building show a crisp colonnaded structure with children running through the arches against a clear backdrop of blue-sky. What greeted me as I approached is a building entangled with ivy, self-seeded trees and a structure whose every component of glazing or fittings have been vandalised or stripped out. Yet the remains stand as a physical manifestation of the agenda established under Mussolini's regime of introducing children from impoverished urban backgrounds to experience the benefits of healthy living.

The original 'colonias marina' was built by charitable Christian organisations in the late nineteenth century. The programme was taken over in the 1920s by the new Fascist state and expanded. Similar to the Kraft durch Freud (Health through Happiness mantra) of which the German holiday camp Rügen on the Baltic Sea, is an example. The Fascist doctrine promoted the idea of Volkskorper, the physical superiority of a new generation. Children were taught military exercises to develop an emotional bond with the Fascist ideology as well as many major industrialists seeing it as an early training regime to create a disciplined new workforce.

The entrance to the 'Colonia' is along an axis which takes you past a gatehouse with a flying concrete roof arriving at an L-shaped colonnade. Here the cloister opens on to a courtyard around an offset pattern of paved gridded lines, which were filled with raked squares of sand, now long gone. The principal entry to the building is to the left as you arrive, where I passed the Chapel, leading to a Crittall glazed façade behind which a ramp running the full height of the building leads to the main dormitories on the upper levels. The extraordinary ramp with banked landings was designed to accommodate up to 600 children spilling out of the dormitories. At each turn, the ramp's gradient takes a sharp drop, akin to a giant Marble Run. At the

Architecture of Leisure

← ↘
The original Crittall windows lead onto the colonnade which wraps around the courtyard. The structure is a mix of insitu-concrete and steel and brick. The spiral staircase leads to the roof terrace.

→ The approach leads you under the arched colonnade which mirrors the flat-roofed colonnade of the accommodation block.

top of the ramp, a minimalist spiral staircase, out of bounds for the children, invites me up to the roof terrace. Ramps were commonly used to accommodate a large number of pupils but also to act as the most efficient way of moving groups of children through the system. Dormitories were all open plan sleeping up to 100 in one space, whilst rows of wash hand basins, squatting toilets and showers were concentrated at the opposite end of the building. This stacked function is expressed on the rear wall with a mosaic of tiles.

The building was designed by the Padovan architect Daniele Calabi, who spent his early years as a young engineering graduate in Paris. Here he absorbed the architecture of Le Corbusier and in particular Marcel Lods. Calabi, born in 1906 was only 34 years when he was awarded the commission by the Opera Nazionale Balilla, (National Youth Organisation). However, on account of his Jewish origin Calabi was exiled to Brazil, under the promulgation of race laws but returned to Italy in 1948. A plaque from 1961 announces the restoration of the building and a large dining hall and theatre were added in the 1970s. The 'colonia' at the time of building was open to the beach, where the film epic 'Death in Venice' was filmed. A recent documentation of the 'Colonia', which appeared in the book *Fascism in Ruins*, published in 2010 described it as – "largely intact with its original kitchen and 'Richard Ginori' crockery service, still present" – so its battered state must be due to recent vandalism over the last decade.

↗
The arched colonnade addresses the generous classrooms with an overall rationalisation of space and all fenestration addressing the courtyard.

Colophon

Publisher Information

The Archive for Rural Contemporary Architecture, ARCA explores interpretations of global landscapes that focus on often marginal and overlooked places. The online archive creates a multi-layered reading of sites and an appreciation of the bleak, the sometimes failed and the uncomfortable. The archive collates and celebrates these strange and often overlooked architectural spaces.

Slacklands 2, expands on the first publication adding to the survey, while opening up more diverse readings of landscapes, which drive aesthetic visions as well as empathy with ecological assemblages. ARCA aims to re-animate the sites that have fallen into disrepair or disuse proposing creative ideas for their reintroduction beyond a limited heritage perspective. As well as bringing them into public consciousness. ARCA acts a roadmap from which other activities develop varying in scale and ambition.

Biographies

Corinna Dean established ARCA, the Archive for Rural Contemporary Architecture, which is an open source archive to encourage participation bottom up, as well as re-engaging cold war structures and other architectural typologies in a rural context. She is engaged in devising cultural projects to bring these sites into the public consciousness through temporary activities such as workshops and creative interpretations and has exhibited this work at the RIBA, Margaret Howell and Sheerness Library. She is a Lecturer in the architecture department at the University of Westminster.

Peter Nencini makes architectural models, typographic forms, workshop props and graphic surfaces. He looks for ways in which animals, plants and people navigate each other in degrees of designed space. In collaboration with writers, designers and fabricators, he has worked with Turf Projects, Eastside Projects Birmingham, Galerie für Zeitgenössische Kunst Leipzig, Walker Art Center Minneapolis, Svenska Tecknare, New York Times, Théâtre National de Toulouse and Salone del Mobile Milan. He teaches at Norwich University of the Arts, previously at Camberwell College of Arts.

Charles Holland is an architect, writer and teacher. He is the Principal of Charles Holland Architects, a design research practice and a Professor of Architecture at the University of Brighton. Before forming CHA, Charles was a founding director of Ordinary Architecture and a director of FAT. Whilst at FAT he was the director in charge of a number of key projects including *A House For Essex*, the practice's collaboration with Grayson Perry.

Thank you to all those involved in the making of the book and Marcus Lee

Open horizons, pages 8–15:
The Valve Station at the Backwater Reservoir, north west Angus; The mock up Atlantic Wall, at Sheriffmuir, Stirlingshire; The runway at the now disused Manston Airport, Kent; The remnants of the Shellness pier on the Isle of Sheppey

Photographs by Corinna Dean
Designed by Ben McLaughlin
Commissioned Artworks by Peter Nencini

Printed and bound in the Netherlands by Unicum, Tilburg and Hexspoor, Boxtel

ISBN 978-1-9161923-0-0